SPITFIRE GIRLS

by Katherine Senior

SAMUEL FRENCH

Copyright © 2025 by Katherine Senior
Cover artwork by Rebecca Pitt
All Rights Reserved

SPITFIRE GIRLS is fully protected under the copyright laws of the British Commonwealth, including Canada, the United States of America, and all other countries of the Copyright Union. All rights, including professional and amateur stage productions, recitation, lecturing, public reading, motion picture, radio broadcasting, television, online/digital production, and the rights of translation into foreign languages are strictly reserved.

ISBN 978-0-573-00076-8

concordtheatricals.co.uk
concordtheatricals.com

FOR PRODUCTION ENQUIRIES

UNITED KINGDOM AND WORLD
EXCLUDING NORTH AMERICA
licensing@concordtheatricals.co.uk

020-7054-7298

NORTH AMERICA
info@concordtheatricals.com
1-866-979-0447

Each title is subject to availability from Concord Theatricals, depending upon country of performance.

CAUTION: Professional and amateur producers are hereby warned that *SPITFIRE GIRLS* is subject to a licensing fee. The purchase, renting, lending or use of this book does not constitute a licence to perform this title(s), which licence must be obtained from the appropriate agent prior to any performance. Performance of this title(s) without a licence is a violation of copyright law and may subject the producer and/or presenter of such performances to penalties. Both amateurs and professionals considering a production are strongly advised to apply to the appropriate agent before starting rehearsals, advertising, or booking a theatre. A licensing fee must be paid whether the title is presented for charity or gain and whether or not admission is charged.

This work is published by Samuel French, an imprint of Concord Theatricals Ltd.

For Professional Rights inquiries contact Concord Theatricals Ltd.

No one shall make any changes in this title for the purpose of production. No part of this book may be reproduced, stored in a retrieval system, scanned, uploaded, or transmitted in any form, by any means, now known or yet to be invented, including mechanical, electronic, digital, photocopying, recording, videotaping, or otherwise, without the prior written permission of the publisher. No one shall share this title, or part of this title, to any social media or file hosting websites.

The moral right of Katherine Senior to be identified as author of this work has been asserted in accordance with Section 77 of the Copyright, Designs and Patents Act 1988.

USE OF COPYRIGHTED MUSIC

A licence issued by Concord Theatricals to perform this play does not include permission to use the incidental music specified in this publication. In the United Kingdom: Where the place of performance is already licensed by the PERFORMING RIGHT SOCIETY (PRS) a return of the music used must be made to them. If the place of performance is not so licensed then application should be made to PRS for Music (www.prsformusic.com). A separate and additional licence from PHONOGRAPHIC PERFORMANCE LTD (www.ppluk.com) may be needed whenever commercial recordings are used. Outside the United Kingdom: Please contact the appropriate music licensing authority in your territory for the rights to any incidental music.

USE OF COPYRIGHTED THIRD-PARTY MATERIALS

Licensees are solely responsible for obtaining formal written permission from copyright owners to use copyrighted third-party materials (e.g., artworks, logos) in the performance of this play and are strongly cautioned to do so. If no such permission is obtained by the licensee, then the licensee must use only original materials that the licensee owns and controls. Licensees are solely responsible and liable for clearances of all third-party copyrighted materials, and shall indemnify the copyright owners of the play(s) and their licensing agent, Concord Theatricals Ltd., against any costs, expenses, losses and liabilities arising from the use of such copyrighted third-party materials by licensees.

IMPORTANT BILLING AND CREDIT REQUIREMENTS

If you have obtained performance rights to this title, please refer to your licensing agreement for important billing and credit requirements.

NOTE

This edition reflects a rehearsal draft of the script and may differ from the final production.

SPITFIRE GIRLS was originally produced by Tilted Wig Productions and MAST Mayflower, Southampton and was first performed at MAST Mayflower, Southampton, on 20th March 2025. The production then toured the UK for ten weeks. The cast and creative team were as follows:

BETT........................Katherine Senior & Rosalind Steele
DOTTY...Laura Matthews
TOM/JIMMY......................................Samuel Tracy
DAD/FRANK......................................Jack Hulland
C.O./JOY..Kirsty Cox

Writer...Katherine Senior
Director & Dramaturg................................Seán Aydon
Designer...Sarah Beaton
Lighting Designer....................................Peter Small
Sound & Composer............................Eamonn O'Dwyer
Movement Director...........................Stephen Moynihan
Video Designer.....................................Tyler Forward
Associate Lighting Designer......................Jodie Underwood
Costume Supervisor..................................Seren Rees
Education Consultant..........................Sinead O'Callaghan
Production Manager..................................Josh Collins
Producer..Matthew Parish
Marketing.......................................Rachel Veniard for
Beth Nichols Marketing
Public Relations.....................................Bright Media
Deputy Stage Manager.............................Lydia Morgan
Company Manager...................................Guy Dennys

The Generate Programme

National Theatre

In aid of

ROYAL BRITISH LEGION

Supported using public funding by
ARTS COUNCIL ENGLAND
LOTTERY FUNDED

SPITFIRE GIRLS was developed with the support of the National Theatre Generate programme and Arts Council England.

Tilted Wig
productions

Tilted Wig has been producing and touring plays across the UK for over seventeen years, with the company now staging at least two tours each year.

Recent productions include national tours: A fresh take on *The School for Scandal* (co-production with Malvern Theatres in association with Theatre by the Lake); a brand new telling of *Frankenstein*; *Around the World in 80 Days* (co-production with York Theatre Royal); *The Legend of Sleepy Hollow* (co-production with Malvern Theatres); *Lady Chatterley's Lover*, *Murder Margaret and Me*, *The Picture of Dorian Gray*, *Great Expectations* (all co-production with Malvern Theatres and Churchill Theatre, Bromley).

Other national tours include: *The Lover, The Private Ear and the Public Eye, The Knack, The Anniversary, Travels with My Aunt, Dumb Show, The Farmer's Wife, Two, Look Back in Anger, The Fair Maid of the West, Hard Times, Born in the Gardens, The Rivals, Charley's Aunt, The Merry Wives of Windsor, She Stoops to Conquer* (all UK tours); *A Christmas Carol* (a co-production with Exeter Northcott for their Christmas season in the main house).

Mayflower Studios

Mayflower, Southampton comprises **Mayflower Theatre** and **Mayflower Studios**.

Mayflower Theatre is the largest presenting theatre on the south coast and is a charitable trust which was set up in 1986 when the Gaumont Theatre was threatened with closure. The theatre reopened in 1987, renamed Mayflower Theatre, and has become one of the most successful independent theatres in the UK with a capacity of 2,271.

Mayflower Studios opened in May 2021 in the city's cultural quarter and is an arts complex comprising a 450-seat theatre and a 130-seat flexible studio.

Under the leadership of Chief Executive Michael Ockwell, over 550,000 annually attend performances across both venues and a further 40,000 take part in the community and outreach programme.

Mayflower were Associate Producers on Music & Lyrics' production of *Fiddler on the Roof* directed by Craig Revel-Horwood and starring Paul Michael-Glaser, the Leicester Curve production of *Beautiful* with Theatre Royal Bath, *Chitty Chitty Bang Bang* with Crossroads Productions and *Titanic the Musical* tours in 2018 and 2023 directed by Thom Southerland. They also produced the mid-scale tour of *The Santa Trap* and *Here Be Monsters* in association with Belfield Slater Productions and *Sizwe Banzi is Dead* with John Pfumojena.

Their co-production of *Fantastically Great Women Who Changed the World* with Kenny Wax Family Entertainment had its world premiere at Mayflower Studios and went on to win the UK Theatre Award for Best Family Entertainment. They co-produced Frantic Assembly's *Metamorphosis*, and in 2024 co-produced *The Lion Inside* and *The Mountaintop* with Leicester Curve and *Coming to England* with Nicoll Entertainment.

They also produce their own Christmas Productions in Mayflower Studios which include *Peter Pan: An Awfully Big Musical Adventure*, *Second Star to the Right*, *Alice: A Musical Adventure in Wonderland*, *A Christmas Carol*, *Down the Rabbit Hole* and *The Wind in the Willows: Toad's Musical Adventure*.

Michael Ockwell | Chief Executive
Alison Harrison | Chief Finance Officer
Matt Goode | Chief Operating Officer
Sara Scott | Creative Director
Thom Southerland | Artistic Director
Jamie Smith | Senior Producer

CAST

KATHERINE SENIOR | Bett

Katherine is an actor, writer and co-founder of Tilted Wig. She also co-founded Creative Cow in 2007. As an actor, she has toured extensively with both companies for over seventeen years performing roles such as Mrs Malaprop in *The Rivals* and Alison in *Look Back in Anger* on major UK tours. She has various audio credits including *Doctor Who – Vortex Ice* and *Unit* (Big Finish).

As a writer, she adapted *A Christmas Carol* for Creative Cow & Exeter Northcott in 2015. *SPITFIRE GIRLS* was developed at the National Theatre Studio as part of their Generate programme. Katherine was recently longlisted for the inaugural WOMEN IN THEATRE LAB as one of the UK's most promising female playwrights.

ROSALIND STEELE | Bett

Theatre includes: *As You Like It* (Pilgrim Players); *Harry Potter and the Cursed Child* (West End); *Fighting Irish* (Belgrade Theatre); *The Provoked Wife* and *Venice Preserved* (RSC); *Shakespeare in Love* (Bath Theatre Royal/Tour); *The Secret Garden* (York Theatre Royal); *The Box of Delights* (Wilton's Music Hall); *William Wordsworth*, *Swallows & Amazons* and *Rogue Herries* (Theatre by the Lake); *Fanny Hill* and *The Lost World* (Bristol Old Vic); *As You Like It* (Oxford Shakespeare Company); *Father Christmas* (The Lyric Hammersmith); *Daisy Pulls it Off* and *Arabian Nights* (Watermill Theatre); *We Didn't Mean to Go to Sea*, *Margaret Catchpole* and *Parkway Dreams* (Eastern Angles); *The Snail and the Whale* (US Tour/Broadway); *The Merchant of Venice* and *A Midsummer Night's Dream* (GB Theatre, UK Tour); *Sam Rose in the Shadows* and *Tim & Light* (Tucked In, UK Tour) and regular appearances at Shakespeare's Globe in the Read not Dead series.

Rosalind is a singer, musical director and composer, and has composed for Read not Dead at the Globe, GB Theatre, Tucked In Productions and Rabble Theatre, for whom she is an associate artist. She has recently written music for a short film.

As a voice artist she has worked on computer games and recorded several audiobooks.

LAURA MATTHEWS | Dotty

Training: Bristol Old Vic Theatre School.

Theatre includes: *The Full Monty* (No 1 UK Tour); *One Man, Two Guvnors* (Theatre Royal Haymarket/National Theatre); *London Assurance* (National Theatre); *Noises Off* (No 1 UK Tour/Ambassadors Theatre Group); *A Brief History of Women* (World Premiere at 59E59 Theater New York/Stephen Joseph Theatre); *The Girl on the Train* (English Theatre Frankfurt); *Henceforward* (UK Tour/Stephen Joseph Theatre); *Taking Steps, No Knowing* (Stephen Joseph Theatre); *Romeo & Juliet, Richard II* (Guildford Shakespeare Company); *Ernest* and *The Pale Moon* (Les Enfants Terribles - Edinburgh Festival/UK Tour/Soho Theatre); *Dick Whittington and His Cat* (Salisbury Playhouse); *Not in the Mood for Quiche Anymore* (Barons Court Theatre); *The Scarlet Pimpernel* (The Egg Bath/Pins & Needles); *The Merchant of Venice, A Midsummer Night's Dream* (GB Theatre, UK Tour); *Select A Quest* (Bristol Old Vic Studio); *We're All In It Together* (Theatre503); *A Month in the Country* (Tobacco Factory).

Television includes: *Babies* (BBC); *Call The Midwife* (Neal Street Productions/BBC); *Eastenders* (BBC); *Doctors* (BBC).

Film includes: *Pride* (Pathé/Proud Films).

Radio includes: *The Shape Of The Table, Falco: Poseidon's Gold* (BBC Radio).

SAMUEL TRACY | Tom/Jimmy

Samuel Tracy is an Actor, Theatremaker and Movement Practitioner currently based in Manchester. His training includes The Royal Academy of Dramatic Art and The BRIT school for Performing Arts and Technology.

Theatre includes: *LIVES* (Lowry Theatre); *The Gruffalo's Child* (West End/National Tour); *The Tempest* (Salisbury Playhouse); *Billy Goats Gruff* (Unicorn Theatre); *Half-Empty Glasses, A Sudden Violent Burst of Rain, The Ultimate Pickle* (Paines Plough Roundabout Season); *WILD* (The Unicorn Theatre); *Romeo & Juliet* (Southwark Playhouse); *Dr. Jekyll & Mr Hyde* (Rose Theatre Kingston); *Sticky* (Southwark Playhouse); *Zigger Zagger* (Wilton's Music Hall); *Orfeo* (Royal Opera House / Roundhouse) and *Because of You* (Hampton Hill Theatre).

Film/Television includes: *Woke Overnight* (BBC)

JACK HULLAND | Dad/Frank

Theatre credits include: *Through the Looking Glass* (Hedgehog Theatre/Fringe Tour); *Travels With My Aunt, The Merry Wives of Windsor, The Rivals, Hard Times, Look Back in Anger, Dumb Show, Lam, The Anniversary, The Knack, The Lover, The Private Ear & The Public Eye* (Creative Cow/UK Tours); *Much Ado About Nothing* (MT Productions/Tour); *The Adventures of a Bear called Paddington* (Upstage Productions/UK Tour); *Robin of the Wood* (Northcott Theatre); *The Taming of the Shrew* (Forest of Dean Theatre Co/Open Air Tour); *Merlin's Dream* (Northcott Theatre); *Jamaica Inn* (Plymouth Theatre Royal/UK Tour); *An Inspector Calls, The Tempest, Cinderella, Macbeth* (Buckhaven Theatre).

Film & TV credits include: *The Passion* (BBC/First Choice), *The Photo Man* (Cavalier Productions), *Wycliffe* (HTV), *Bugs* (BBC/Carnival Films), *The Vet* (BBC/Ikona Films).

Vocal credits include: *Made in Heaven* (BBC Radio 4), *Daddy* (Channel Four/Black Watch/Stephen Cavalier).

Training: Cygnet Training Theatre, Exeter.

KIRSTY COX | C.O./Joy

Kirsty Cox trained at the Royal Conservatoire of Scotland. Her recent theatre work includes *Christmas Present and Correct, Houdini's Greatest Escape, Crimes on Centre Court, A Christmas Getaway, Crimes, Camera, Action* and *Crimes on the Nile* (New Old Friends); *Our Church* (The Watermill Theatre); *Down To Earth, I Believe in Unicorns, Apple John, The Boy Who Climbed Into The Moon* and *Olive and the Dream Train* (Theatre Alibi); *The Odyssey* and *Medusa* (Bristol Old Vic); *1599: A Year in the Life of William Shakespeare* and *Shakespeare's Worst* (Bristol Shakespeare Festival); *The Macbeth Curse* (Prime Theatre/Bolton Octagon); *The Last Post* (Kilter Theatre) and the one woman show *Stalin's Daughter* (Blue Brook Productions). She is a regular performer with street theatre company, The Naturals, and the comedy improvisation group, Instant Wit. She has recorded numerous audiobooks and also radio drama including Enchanted Isle for BBC Radio 4. Her film and television experience includes *Trollied* (Sky TV), commercials for Toolstation and Visit Wales, and several independent feature films.

CREATIVE

KATHERINE SENIOR | Writer

Katherine is an actor, writer and co-founder of Tilted Wig. As an actor, she has toured extensively for over seventeen years performing roles such as Mrs Malaprop in *The Rivals* and Alison in *Look Back in Anger* on major UK tours. She has various audio credits including *Doctor Who - Vortex Ice* and *Unit* (Big Finish).

As a writer, she adapted *A Christmas Carol* for Creative Cow & Exeter Northcott in 2015. *SPITFIRE GIRLS* was developed at the National Theatre Studio as part of their Generate programme. Katherine was recently longlisted for the inaugural WOMEN IN THEATRE LAB as one of the UK's most promising female playwrights.

SEÁN AYDON | Director & Dramaturg

Seán is a director, writer and dramaturg who has worked at theatres across the UK. He is also artistic director for Tilted Wig Productions. Seán has adapted and directed national tours of *The Picture of Dorian Gray* and *Frankenstein*. Other directing credits include *The School for Scandal* (National Tour), *Love Lab* (Seven Dials Playhouse) and *Richard III* (Rosemary Branch Islington, nominated for Best Director in The Stage Debut Awards). He was also assistant director to Derek Bond on the world premiere of Tom Fletcher's *The Christmasaurus* at the Hammersmith Apollo. Having originally trained as an actor at Manchester School of Theatre, he worked as an actor for several years, playing theatres including the Royal Exchange (Manchester), Liverpool Everyman & the Mercury Theatre (Colchester), as well as playing Pip in the UK tour of *Great Expectations*. New writing and dramaturgy have always been a key part Seán's work - alongside being a script reader for the Finborough theatre for several years, he has worked on new writing events at the Young Vic, the Old Vic, the NT Studio, the Arts Theatre (Leicester Square) and Theatre 503. Seán is a permanent acting lecturer at Manchester School of Theatre (MMU), where he has directed public productions of *Husbands & Sons*, *Mr Burns* and *Hedda Gabler* with the third-year actors.

SARAH BEATON | Designer

Sarah is a performance designer & visual dramaturge. She studied Design for Stage at The Central School of Speech & Drama, graduating in 2011 with First Class Honours. Later that year she was awarded The Linbury Prize for Stage Design. From 2015-2016 she was the Designer on Attachment at The Old Vic. Her work has been exhibited at The National Theatre, World Stage Design (Cardiff), the V&A and World Stage Design (Taiwan).

Theatre work includes *The Lightest Element*, *The Harmony Test*, *Nineteen Gardens*, *Mother Christmas* (Hampstead Theatre); *Carmen* (Scottish Opera); *The Merchant of Venice* (Shakespeare's Globe); *Babur in London* (Sadler's Wells); *Wild East* (Young Vic); *MUM* (Plymouth Theatre Royal/Soho); *Faust* (Altes Schauspielhaus, Germany); *La Bohème* (Longborough Festival Opera); *The Human Voice* (Gate); *Building the Wall* (Park Theatre); *Crocodiles* (Manchester Royal Exchange); *Possession*, *Great Apes*, *The Double Act* (Arcola); *Rise* (Old Vic); *In Event of Moon Disaster* (Theatre503); *One Who Wants to Cross* (Finborough Theatre); *Diary of a Madman* (Sherman Theatre); *Mix the Play* (Old Vic); *Missing*, *Run*, *Gap in the Light* (Engineer Theatre Collective).

PETER SMALL | Lighting Designer

Peter is an Offie and Theatre & Technology Award nominated lighting designer working across mediums such as theatre, dance, opera and immersive. In 2018 Peter was nominated for two Off West End Best Lighting Awards for *Black Mountain* and *A Girl in School Uniform (Walks in to a Bar)*.

Credits include: *Kathy & Stella Solve A Murder* (The Ambassadors Theatre in the West End, Bristol Old Vic, HOME Manchester & Edinburgh Fringe); *King Stakh's Wild Hunt* (The Barbican); *Baby Reindeer* (Bush Theatre & Edinburgh Fringe); *All or Nothing* (West End & on tour); *What Remains Of Us* (Bristol Old Vic); *KS6: Small Forward* (The Barbican & La MaMa, New York); *The School for Scandal* (UK Tour); *Lady Chatterley's Lover* (UK Tour); *Orlando* (59E59 New York); *Shrek The Musical* and *My Fair Lady* (Mercury Theatre, Colchester); *Cinderella* (Queens Theatre Hornchurch); *Sylvia* and *Nunsense* (both at English Theatre Frankfurt); *Twelfth Night* (Kew Gardens); *58th Street*, *The Great Murder Mystery*, *The Greatest Night of the Jazz Age* and *The Great Christmas Feast* (all with The Lost Estate); *The Ritual Slaughter of Gorge Mastromas*, *The Caucasian Chalk Circle*, *The Priory* and *A Skull in Connemara* (all at the Dailes Theatre, Latvia).

EAMONN O'DWYER | Sound & Composer

Eamonn O'Dwyer is an award-winning composer-lyricist of Guyanese-Irish heritage. His work spans genres from live orchestral to electronica, contemporary musical theatre, film, video games & attractions. He is an Associate of the Royal Academy of Music, and to date his works have been performed in the US, Russia, Australia and Japan.

Other theatrical credits include: *Never Let Me Go* (Rose Theatre Kingston & UK Tour); *The History Boys* (Bath Theatre Royal & UK Tour); *The Lion Inside* (Unicorn & UK Tour); *Guy Fawkes* (York Theatre Royal); *The Rise & Fall of Little Voice* (UK Tour); *Brief Encounter* (Watermill); *Lady Chatterley's Lover* (UK Tour); *Twelfth Night* and *Henry V* (Shakespeare's Rose Theatre, York); *Mrs Beeton Says...* (Bristol Old Vic Theatre School); *The Legend of Sleepy Hollow* (NYMT, The Other Palace); *The Comedy of Errors* and *Julius Caesar Re-imagined* (RSC, Swan); *Flesh & Bone* (National Theatre Studio); *Grimm Tales* and *Peter Pan* (Chichester Festival Theatre); *Jeeves & Wooster* (Barn, Cirencester); *Stones In His Pockets* (Dukes, Lancaster); *The Glass Menagerie* (Theatre Chipping Norton); *The Snow Queen, Hansel & Gretel, The Wind in the Willows, The Lion, The Witch & The Wardrobe*, all for the Rose Theatre in Kingston.

STEPHEN MOYNIHAN | Movement Director

Stephen is an Irish movement director and choreographer. After graduating from London Contemporary Dance School, he performed with renowned choreographers such as Damien Jalet and Akram Khan, including at the London 2012 Olympic Opening Ceremony. His work spans theatre, opera, and fashion, collaborating with companies such as Attic Projects, Dumbworld, London College of Fashion, and Raymond Gubbay at the Royal Albert Hall. In film and television, he honed his movement craft alongside leading movement directors, working with Alex Reynolds and Polly Bennett, among others. Stephen's recent screen work includes choreography for *Ted Lasso* (Apple TV+), movement coaching for *House of the Dragon* (HBO Max), as well as working on *The Witcher* (Netflix) and *The Northman* with director Robert Eggers. He has extensive experience creating creature movement and motion capture, contributing to productions such as *His Dark Materials* (BBC), *The Mummy*, and *Aquaman 2*. A recipient of the DanceWeb Scholarship at Impulstanz in Vienna, Stephen has also served on the Dance Panel for the Olivier Awards. His theatre credits with Tilted Wig include *Frankenstein* and *The School for Scandal*, and he is excited to return for *SPITFIRE GIRLS*.

TYLER FORWARD | Video Designer

As Designer, theatre includes: *The 25th Annual Putnam County Spelling Bee* (Mack) *The Legends of Them* (Royal Court) *A MidSummer Night's Dream* (Backstage), *Turn of The Screw* (Queens Theatre Hornchurch); *G* (Royal Court); *Dorian The Musical* (Southwark Playhouse); *Sunday In Park with George* (Mack); *Diana The Musical Concert* (Eventim Apollo); *Trompe L'Oiel* (The Other Palace); *Loserville* (Blackheath Halls); *Our House* (The Albany); *No Man's Island, Redemption, Mission* (The Big House); *Play, The Games* (P&O Arvia); *Silence* (Donmar/Tara); *Roles We'll Never Play* (Lyric), *Close Quarters* (RADA); *Thoroughly Modern Millie* (Electric); *Nor Woman Neither* (Tristan Bates); *Macbeth* (Vanbrugh); *Stoning Mary* (George Bernard Shaw).

LYDIA MORGAN | Deputy Stage Manager

Lydia is a freelance Stage Manager who trained at Bristol Old Vic Theatre School. Previous credits include: ASM on *In The Night Garden* (UK Tour), Stage Manager on *Well Done, Mummy Penguin* (The Arc), ASM on *The Changeling* (Southwark Playhouse) and Technical Stage Manager on *Life Before You* (The Alma Tavern Theatre). Lydia is also a technician who works at The Tobacco Factory Theatre in Bristol.

GUY DENNYS | Company Manager

Guy trained as an actor at Cygnet Theatre in Exeter and at the National Youth Theatre of Great Britain. After his training, Guy went on to work in various capacities throughout the creative arts. Having worked both on and off-stage with Tilted Wig, Guy is delighted to be returning as Company Manager on *SPITFIRE GIRLS*.

Theatre credits include: *The School for Scandal* (Tilted Wig/UK Tour); *Lady Chatterley's Lover* (Tilted Wig/UK Tour); *Don Carlos* (Ara Theatre Company/Exeter Northcott/ Rose Theatre Kingston); *A Christmas Carol* (Creative Cow/ Exeter Northcott); *Macbeth* (Devil You Know Theatre); *The Browning Version* (Common Players); *Medea* (Four of Swords); *Around the World in 80 Days* (Tilted Wig/UK Tour); *Frankenstein* (Tilted Wig/ UK Tour).

MATTHEW PARISH | Producer

Matthew is co-founder of Tilted Wig and has been a producer for over eighteen years. Having trained as an actor he has worked in various capacities on all of Tilted Wig's major UK tours as an actor, company manager, production manager and producer collaborating with regional venues including Malvern Theatres, York Theatre Royal, Theatre by the Lake and Churchill Theatre, Bromley. He's delighted to be teaming up with MAST Mayflower on this premiere production of *Spitfire Girls* and is working on various projects for 2026 and beyond.

JOSH COLLINS | Production Manager

Josh is a freelance Production Manager working across opera and theatre. After graduating from The Guildhall School of Music and Drama with The Gold Medal he worked in electrics throughout the West End, in Asia, and at Hampstead Theatre. Josh now production manages for various companies across London and further afield. Recent Production Management credits include: *The Double Act* (Arcola Theatre), *An Interrogation* (Hampstead Theatre), *Christmas in Exeter Street* (Farnham Maltings), *King James* (Hampstead Theatre), *Maria de Rudenz* (Battersea Arts Centre), *Visit from an Unknown Woman* (Hampstead Theatre) and *An Actor Convalescing in Devon* (Hampstead Theatre).

SEREN REES | Costume Supervisor

Seren is a recent graduate of the Arts University Bournemouth studying Costume.

Previously she has worked on *The Book of Mormon* at the Prince of Wales Theatre (Dresser), *Singing in the Rain* at Kilworth House (Supervisor's Assistant), *Dear England* at the National Theatre (Dresser), *Dirty Dancing* UK West End and on Tour (Wardrobe Assistant), and *Cinderella* with Crossroad Pantomimes (Alterations Assistant).

ACKNOWLEDGMENTS

Thank you to MAST Mayflower Studios and Poole Lighthouse for providing a week of development in 2023 and to the National Theatre Generate Programme and all the New Work team for providing an invaluable week of development at the NT Studio in the summer of 2024 and making our little company feel so valued.

Thank you to the creatives who have been an invaluable part of developing the play over the last three years: Michele O'Brien, Daniel Goode, Dale Mathurin, Kate Pasco, Vicki-Jo Eva, Dan Gaisford and the cast of the 2025 production. Special thanks to Bethan Nash for being there from the beginning and for being so integral to the development.

Thank you to Mark Green for his deep knowledge of the ATA and aviation, Marie-Clare at Sunflower Thinking, The Royal British Legion and Arts Council England. Thanks to Candy Adkins (daughter of ATA pilot Jackie Moggridge) for sharing her Mum's archive. Special thanks to Mary Ellis, one of the ATA pilots based at Hamble, who I had the pleasure of chatting with over a cup of tea on the Isle of Wight in 2017 when she was one hundred years old.

Thank you to Seán Aydon for believing in the piece and helping me shape it into this play. Finally, thanks so much to Susy for all the proofing and to my three sons and Matt, who always keep the noise at peak level for writing.

CHARACTERS

BETT – a woman in her early forties who also plays herself in her mid-twenties

DOTTY – a woman in her mid-twenties

DAD – a middle aged man, also plays **FRANK**

FRANK – a middle aged man

TOM – a West Indian man in his twenties, also plays **JIMMY**

JIMMY – a man of any age

COMMANDING OFFICER – Commanding Officer of NO. 15 Ferry Pool (Hamble-on-Solent), female. Also plays **JOY**.

JOY – A pilot for the ATA, female.

GROUND CREW – Doubled by **TOM**.

INSTRUCTOR – Doubled by **DAD**.

SETTING

The action of the play moves between The Spitfire Pub, Bett & Dotty's farmhouse kitchen, Hamble Ferry Pool, and another pub.

TIME

The play moves between 1943–45 and New Year's Eve 1959.

AUTHOR'S NOTE

A forward slash (/) marks the point of interruption in overlapping dialogue.

A dash (–) marks the point of interruption that cuts off the dialogue.

An ellipsis (…) marks the point where the character cannot finish the thought.

Where the dialogue is broken to the next line, even by a single word, it is the intention that the thought is broken/difficult to say.

ACT ONE

Scene One

(A pub. New Year's Eve. 1959. Around five p.m. and it's raining hard.)

(Inside the pub, it's very dimly lit. There are pictures everywhere; photos and illustrations of wartime aircraft.* Above the door, there's a stained glass window that says "THE SPITFIRE" and faces out.)

(In the corner, there is a small Christmas Tree with a gesture of lights and decorations. Next to it, is a well-worn cardboard box. A wire recorder sits on the bar. A banner hangs reading "Welcome 1960".)

*(A **WOMAN** in her early forties enters from behind the bar and quickly fills a dog bowl with water from a pint glass, whistling as she does so.)*

(Without breaking stride, she deposits the glass on the bar and heads over to the cardboard box. She takes out various bits of decoration, tossing tinsel onto the floor.)

---

* A licence to produce *Spitfire Girls* does not include a licence to publicly display any third-party or copyrighted images. Licensees must acquire rights for any copyrighted images or create their own.

(Suddenly, something makes her stop. She takes a breath before slowly lifting a reel out of the bottom of the box.)

(After a moment, she moves over to the player and places the reel on the recorder, threading the wire carefully. She takes another moment before pressing play.)

(The machine plays a recording of people counting down to New Year followed by a single female voice singing "Auld Lang Syne".)*

(There is a knock at the door. Pause. Another knock. Pause.)

*(**BETT** is motionless.)*

*(Another knock. **BETT** looks at the door.)*

*(She turns off the recording, takes off the reel, puts it back in the box, shoving the decorations on top. **BETT** takes a moment, looks at her wristwatch, and then moves to the door. Unlocks and opens it. There's no one there. A moment and then…)*

BETT. Bloody hell!

FRANK. I was just going round the back.

BETT. We're not open, Frank.

FRANK. It's chucking it down out here / love.

BETT. I don't care. We're not open till six.

FRANK. I won't be no trouble / Bett.

---

* A licence to produce *Spitfire Girls* does not include a performance licence for any third-party or copyrighted recordings. Licensees should create their own.

BETT. That's not true, is it?

FRANK. I can just perch on me stool / there.

BETT. I've got too much to sort / out

FRANK. I'm sodden / through

BETT. I don't need you yapping in my ear.

FRANK. What ever happened to "goodwill to all men"?

BETT. I only know "goodwill to good men", Frank.

FRANK. That's below the belt.

BETT. And women for that matter.

FRANK. Steady.

BETT. We'll be open before you know it and you can drink the place dry.

FRANK. Come on, Bett.

BETT. Bye, Frank.

> *(She closes the door on him and locks up.)*

(Sotto.) Bloody nightmare.

> *(She returns to the box and puts the remaining decs back in. Tucks the lid under and over with care and picks up the box. Another knock.* **BETT** *looks to the door but ignores it. She puts the cardboard box out of sight. Another knock.)*

He won't give up, will he?

> *(She unlocks and opens the door. Beat.)*

DOTTY. Hello.

> *(Beat.)*

BETT. You.

(Beat.)

BETT. Come in, come in. It's lashing it down. You must be wet through –

DOTTY. *(Entering.)* Not too bad, actually.

BETT. I best just...sorry.

> (**BETT** *locks the door again.*)

Safe and sound.

> *(She bolts it. They smile.)*

So.

DOTTY. So.

> *(Beat.)*

BETT. Yes. So. Here we are.

DOTTY. Yes.

BETT. Raining cats and dogs, isn't it?

DOTTY. Yes.

BETT. Shall I take your...?

DOTTY. No, thank you.

BETT. Of course. It takes a while for this place to warm up, I'm afraid.

> *(Beat.)*

1960, eh?

DOTTY. 1960.

BETT. Can't believe it, really.

DOTTY. No.

> *(Beat.)*

BETT. Drink?

DOTTY. No, thank you.

BETT. Nothing at all?

>(**DOTTY** *shakes her head.*)

Mind if I do?

DOTTY. Of course not. Go ahead.

>(**BETT** *goes behind the bar.*)

BETT. You sure...?

>(**DOTTY** *shakes her head and watches* **BETT** *as she sorts her drink. Pause.*)

DOTTY. What's her name?

>(*Beat.*)

Or is it a he?

>(**DOTTY** *gestures to the dog bowl.*)

BETT. Oh. Yes. She. Dorothy. She's called Dorothy.

DOTTY. Ah. Lovely.

BETT. Yes. She's a frightened ol' thing now. She used to be a permanent fixture out here but she got a bit fed up with the clientele; she's far higher standards than me.

DOTTY. Have you had her long?

BETT. A fair while. I got her from the Blue Cross not long after it all finished.

DOTTY. Gosh.

BETT. Oh yes, she's geriatric. I'll entice her out here later with a mince pie.

DOTTY. *(Half laughing.)* Do dogs eat mince pies?

BETT. Dorothy's no ordinary dog.

    *(**DOTTY** smiles.)*

Cheers.

DOTTY. Cheers.

    *(**BETT** takes out a cigarette and offers to **DOTTY**, but she declines.)*

BETT. Really?

    (She lights it.)

You used to smoke. You used to drink.

DOTTY. I know.

BETT. You could drink most of the girls under the table.

    *(**DOTTY** smiles.)*

Still, that was a long time ago. You haven't changed. Not really.

DOTTY. Neither have you.

BETT. I don't believe that one bit.

DOTTY. You haven't.

BETT. I'm an old hag. This place should be called "The Old Hag".

DOTTY. Oh, come on…

BETT. No, I'm happy with that. Really. It gives me a certain weight. No one messes with The Old Hag at The Spit.

DOTTY. Well, I wouldn't. But then, I never did.

BETT. I remember having plenty of wrangles with you.

DOTTY. Yes, but there weren't many you lost.

BETT. Maybe.

(Beat.)

DOTTY. You've some wonderful pictures. Is this all you?

BETT. What do you think?

DOTTY. I thought so. It's like stepping inside your mind.

BETT. Huh. Tread carefully, eh?

DOTTY. Always.

(Beat.)

We used to talk about running a pub, didn't we?

BETT. Did we?

DOTTY. Yes. We said we'd call it "The Queen's Head-ache".

BETT. I should have used that. Why didn't I use that?

DOTTY. Is that why you have this place?

BETT. I honestly don't remember us talking about it. It must have been a thousand years ago.

DOTTY. Yes, I suppose so.

(Pause.)-

Gosh, look at us.

BETT. Footloose –

BETT & DOTTY. And fancied a G&T!

DOTTY. The magnificent wonder that was The Pavilion.

BETT. And the magnificent men that frequented it.

DOTTY. What was that fella's name? On the left there?

BETT. I miss that place.

DOTTY. This one.

BETT. Oh, he had the darkest eyes.

DOTTY. Flew a B17.

BETT. And enormous feet.

DOTTY. Woody!

BETT. Yes. Woody. "Woody Won't He".

(They laugh.)

DOTTY. Always guaranteed a fun night at The Pav.

BETT. I like to think I offer the same kind of entertainment here.

DOTTY. Oh?

BETT. Yes. Come twenty-one hundred hours we're rammed to the rafters with plucky young pilots.

DOTTY. I'm sure.

BETT. Trouble is, there's a point in the evening when it's like hiking on the heath through thick fog; we have to switch the fans on to see everyone's heads.

*(**DOTTY** has spotted a sketch of a Spitfire.)*

Not *quite* The Pavilion, is it?

DOTTY. –

BETT. That reminds me, I best get this thing set up for tonight. Do you mind?

*(**BETT** moves to the wire recorder and places a reel on it carefully. **DOTTY** stares at the sketch.)*

Apart from Dorothy, this is my closest friend. Wouldn't be without it.

DOTTY. This sketch –

BETT. I mean, it's still bloody fiddly as hell / but –

DOTTY. This picture / here –

BETT. Which one?

DOTTY. *(Sotto.)* Which one. This one.

BETT. Just a / sec.

DOTTY. The little Spit.

BETT. Hang on, let me just…

> (**DOTTY** *waits patiently.*)

Bloody thing.

> (**DOTTY** *waits.*)

If I'm not careful it'll snap and that'll be the end of it.

DOTTY. *(Sotto.)* It's not the only one.

BETT. It's antique; you have to be very patient.

DOTTY. Oh, I am.

> *(1940s music plays.*)*

BETT. Listen to that. Worth the wait, isn't it?

> (**DOTTY** *looks at* **BETT.***)*

Drink?

DOTTY. I –

BETT. Sorry, force of habit. Mind if I?

DOTTY. Please.

> (**BETT** *moves to the bar and makes a drink.*)

So, this picture.

BETT. Which one?

---

* A licence to produce *Spitfire Girls* does not include a performance licence for any third-party or copyrighted music. Licensees should create an original composition or use music in the public domain. For further information, please see the Music Use Note on page iii.

DOTTY. When did you get it?

BETT. Oh. I don't know.

DOTTY. Where did you get it?

BETT. Do you know, I collect so much tat. If I see something that looks like it needs rescuing, I take it home.

DOTTY. Is that right?

BETT. Be careful. If you stay here too long, I'll have you measured up and on display in the saloon bar.

(**DOTTY** *just about manages a smirk.*)

I'm not joking. I've got regulars stuffed and hanging in the urinals.

DOTTY. You always were very good at avoiding the subject. So, this / picture

BETT. Gosh, we're still very stubborn, aren't we?

DOTTY. Yes we are.

BETT. What. What would you like to know about that picture?

DOTTY. Why you have it.

BETT. I like it.

DOTTY. Right.

BETT. I like the feeling of freedom it offers me.

DOTTY. Does it?

BETT. Yes.

DOTTY. It looks ominous. To me. Foreboding.

BETT. Well, I suppose that's the power of art; everyone sees something different.

DOTTY. Did someone draw it for you?

BETT. It's just a picture. I have hundreds of them.

DOTTY. Did they?

BETT. Yes, I think someone did.

DOTTY. Who?

BETT. I don't remember. And do you know what, I think I'm done talking about it.

DOTTY. Why?

BETT. Why? Because I have spent too long fretting about the past. Wondering if things could have been... If I had acted differently. Things are better left.

> *(Dance hall music plays from the recorder as if from a distant memory.*)*

DOTTY. *(Referring to the picture of them.)* We signed up that day.

BETT. Did we?

DOTTY. Yes, I think so.

BETT. I don't remember.

DOTTY. That's why we went to The Pav two nights in a row.

BETT. We did?

DOTTY. Uh-huh.

BETT. Dear Lord.

DOTTY. Surely you can remember that hangover?

> *(Mocking.)* You were a bear with a very sore head. I made you endless cups of tea? He blew his top because we ate all the bread? He'd just bought that newfangled toaster and I kept –

BETT & DOTTY. Burning the toast!

---

* A licence to produce *Spitfire Girls* does not include a performance licence for any third-party or copyrighted music. Licensees should create an original composition or use music in the public domain. For further information, please see the Music Use Note on page iii.

(They smile.)

DOTTY. *(Lost in the photo.)* That dance hall certainly saw some sights.

BETT. Didn't it just. Another lifetime.

(Beat.)

But oh, how we *loved* to dance.

DOTTY. That's what you call it, is it?

BETT. Oh, you're so very funny.

DOTTY. I always feared for my life.

*(**BETT** shoves her and **DOTTY** giggles.)*

Sometimes. In the darkness. If you listened very carefully. You could hear my little toes screaming in terror.

BETT. Hilarious.

DOTTY. Woody He Won't He wished he'd worn his steel toe-caps that / night.

BETT. Shut up.

(They look at each other and smile. The music has changed to something recognisable, perhaps "their" song.)

DOTTY. Well...?

BETT. ...Well...?

*(**DOTTY** bows in the most ridiculous way, then holds out her hand.)*

No.

DOTTY. May I have this dance?

BETT. Absolutely not.

*(**DOTTY** begins her part of the routine, at first small, then building up.)*

God help me.

DOTTY. *(Offering again.)* Madam?

*(**BETT** watches in dismay knowing that there is no way out of it. It reaches the point where it's **BETT**'s turn and she is pulled into the dance. We watch the two of them dance with joy, verve and utter abandon as they're transported back to the dance hall of 1943.)*

Scene Two

>*(Spring of 1943. The kitchen of a farmhouse, with a hefty wooden table at its heart.* **BETT**, *now in her late twenties, is seated at the table, cradling her head in her hands.* **DOTTY**, *some years younger, places a steaming cup of tea in front of* **BETT**.*)*

DOTTY. You were dancing so fast, I thought he was going to catapult you into the bar!

BETT. How very dare you! He could barely keep up with me.

DOTTY. Did you get his name?

BETT. I am not having this conversation with you.

DOTTY. Why? *(Mocking.)* Does your head hurt?

BETT. It is a *little* sore, yes.

DOTTY. From where you hit the bar physically or metaphorically?

BETT. Shut up.

>*(Beat.)*

DOTTY. What's that you're doing?

BETT. Saw an ad.

DOTTY. An ad? What sort of ad?

BETT. In here. Thought I'd apply.

DOTTY. Oh?

BETT. Ohhhh.

DOTTY. Looks dangerous.

BETT. I hope so.

DOTTY. Can anyone answer it then?

BETT. Looks like it. As long as you're tall, fit and moderately healthy.

DOTTY. So why are you applying?

> (**BETT** *throws a different newspaper at her –* **DOTTY** *laughs and hovers over her.*)

Might give it a go myself.

BETT. I'm not sure that's a good idea.

DOTTY. Why not? I'm far more athletic than you and as we all know, at least half an inch taller.

BETT. You've never even driven a car!

DOTTY. *(Looking at the ad.)* That doesn't appear to be in the criteria. *(Picking up the notepad and pen.)* Oooh, you're at the arse end of the age range, aren't you?

> (**BETT** *swings for* **DOTTY** *but she ducks out of the way.*)

DOTTY. Who do you address it to?

BETT. I really don't think you should.

DOTTY. *(Writing.)* "Air Transport Auxiliary"...

BETT. Dot, I don't think you should.

DOTTY. Of course you don't. You wouldn't.

BETT. Dad'll lose his rag when he finds out we've both applied.

DOTTY. Then he shouldn't leave his stuff lying around willy-nilly, then, should he?

BETT. We can't both up sticks and leave him.

DOTTY. You stay then.

> *(Beat.)*

Well, why should *I*?

BETT. Because I need this. Think I've done my bit here.

DOTTY. Wow. I never asked you to, you know.

BETT. Oh come on, I didn't mean you. I'd do it all over again for you in a heartbeat, Dotty. But I need this.

DOTTY. So do I. Please. So do I.

BETT. He'll hit the roof.

DOTTY. Probably. He'll blow his top and then get back to his stinkin' pigs.

Come on. *(Lord Kitchener to* **BETT***.)* "Your country needs you".

*(***BETT** *sniggers.)*

(Again.) "And your sister".

BETT. You're a clown.

DOTTY. *(She shows her bicep.)* "We can do it!"

BETT. Any more?

DOTTY. "Dig for Vic–"

BETT. Alright!

DOTTY. Propaganda, eh? Works a treat.

BETT. It's not a jolly though, you know that? We'll be joining the effort.

DOTTY. I know, Bett.

BETT. And I won't be able to protect you.

DOTTY. Bliss!

BETT. *(Clutching at straws.)* Ah, there's only one envelope left.

DOTTY. Then we'll double up. Give here. It'll be an adventure, Betty. Just me, you and the big blue.

(**BETT** *gives in and hands her the envelope.* **DOTTY** *can't contain her excitement as she puts her application in.*)

BETT. Promise me, if we do get in, you'll behave.

DOTTY. I'll behave, Mum. Promise.

(**BETT** *looks at* **DOTTY**.)

Sorry.

BETT. Why do you say that?

DOTTY. It was just a joke.

BETT. It's not funny.

DOTTY. Sorry.

(**DOTTY** *pulls a sad face which turns into a smile that pulls* **BETT** *back onside.*)

Pav again tonight, dear?

BETT. Oh, I don't know. I'm not feeling too clever, I have to say.

DOTTY. Oh, go on. It may be the last time we can enjoy ourselves if we get lucky with this. We'll be tied to a cockpit forever more…

(**BETT** *gives in.*)

BETT. Alright.

DOTTY. Yes! And Tom said he would be there.

BETT. Super…

DOTTY. Oh Bett. I know he's not your favourite person but please make an effort to humour him.

BETT. Mmm… He's fickle, shall we say?

DOTTY. Well, even fickle is worth a tickle.

BETT. What?

DOTTY. I don't know.

>*(Beat.)*

BETT. What's that smell? Smells like…

BETT & DOTTY. Toast!

BETT. You've really got the hang of that machine, haven't you!?

DOTTY. Shut up. I can just pop some more on.

BETT. No, no. Give it here. I love it when it tastes like the earth's core.

DOTTY. Never mind the toast, it'll be the dance floor we're burning up tonight, me old gal!

>*(She spins* **BETT** *around. They laugh and dance as loud dance hall music plays.*)*

---

* A licence to produce *Spitfire Girls* does not include a performance licence for any third-party or copyrighted music. Licensees should create an original composition or use music in the public domain. For further information, please see the Music Use Note on page iii.

Scene Three

(1943. Later that night. The Pavilion. They have to shout to be heard.)

DOTTY. Did you get his name?

BETT. Woody.

DOTTY. Who?

BETT. WOODY!

DOTTY. Woody? And would you?

BETT. Oh, you're so smutty.

DOTTY. I am not. I am "a lady".

BETT. Says who?

DOTTY. Tom.

BETT. He must be mad, as well as incredibly short.

DOTTY. We're the same height if I don't wear heels.

BETT. Yes, and if he doesn't wear heels?

DOTTY. You're very mean. I'm off to the lavvy.

(Last orders bell.)

BETT. Right-o. From the look of that queue, you might not make it back. I'll get us another.

*(She mimes a drink. **DOTTY** goes. **BETT** lights a cigarette.)*

(The music quietens. They can talk normally.)

Gin and tonic, please. Two.

*(**TOM** enters.)*

TOM. Make that three.

BETT. Good grief, Tom! I wish you wouldn't do that.

TOM. The element of surprise; I need the practice.

BETT. *(Smiling.)* I s'pose so.

> *(Beat.)*

Dot's just nipped to the... *(Gestures.)*

TOM. How you been?

BETT. Fine. You?

TOM. Fine. Dandy.

> *(He offers a cigarette.)*

Want one?

> *(**BETT** shows she has one.)*

Alright.

> *(He moves in.)*

Do you have a light?

BETT. Have you had to ask for a light for every cigarette you've smoked tonight?

> *(**TOM** smiles and takes out his lighter.)*

Dotty will be back soon.

TOM. Alright.

BETT. She's only gone to spend a penny.

TOM. Alright.

BETT. You really are a man of few words, aren't you?

TOM. I'm thinking.

BETT. Woah, steady there.

TOM. Ha, that's a joke.

BETT. Well, only if you laugh.

TOM. *(He laughs.)* You're a funny girl.

BETT. Yes, it has been said.

TOM. You make me smile, Bett.

> *(Beat.)*

What?

BETT. Dotty. She's really keen on you, Tom.

TOM. And are you?

BETT. What?

TOM. Are you keen on me?

BETT. I…

> *(Beat.)*

That doesn't matter.

TOM. Oh?

> *(They look at each other. The three drinks are served.* **TOM** *reaches for his money.)*

BETT. No, no. I'll get it.

> *(She hands over the money.)*

Thanks.

> *(Beat.)*

Chin-chin.

> *(They drink.)*

TOM. That fella you were dancing with…

BETT. Woody.

TOM. He's bad news, you know.

BETT. Is he?

> *(Beat.)*

Tom. She's head over heels for you. Don't hurt her kind, kind heart.

TOM. Alright.

BETT. Promise?

> *(**TOM** crosses his heart.)*

TOM. An' hope to die.

BETT. Well, don't do that.

> *(They smile at each other.)*

Don't disappear as soon as we leave either.

TOM. I'm not going nowhere, I just got myself a drink.

BETT. Very funny, you know what I mean.

TOM. Not a clue.

BETT. When we leave for the ATA.

TOM. For the what now?

BETT. She hasn't told you?

TOM. No.

BETT. Ah.

TOM. What's the ATA?

> *(**DOTTY** returns.)*

DOTTY. Why, hello…

TOM. Hello.

DOTTY. Everything alright?

BETT. Yup. Everything's fine…

TOM. ...and dandy.

BETT. Right! It's my turn for the Pav Pelvic Floor Challenge. Wish me luck!

> (**BETT** *goes.* **TOM** *hands* **DOTTY** *her drink. They clink.*)

DOTTY. Chin-chin.

TOM. Bottoms up.

> *(Beat.)*

DOTTY. Tom –

TOM. What's the ATA?

DOTTY. Ah.

TOM. Ah.

DOTTY. I was going to tell you.

TOM. Of course.

DOTTY. I was.

TOM. Uh-huh.

DOTTY. I just didn't quite know how.

TOM. Give it a whirl.

> *(Beat.)*

DOTTY. Bett and I have applied to the Air Transport Auxiliary.

TOM. Well, that was easy.

DOTTY. Shut up.

TOM. Doing what, exactly?

DOTTY. Flying aeroplanes around the country.

TOM. As a pilot?

DOTTY. Sort of.

TOM. A sort of pilot?

DOTTY. Well, we'd be ferrying aeroplanes.

TOM. On a ferry?

DOTTY. Oh come on.

> *(Beat.)*

Surely you've heard of the ATA?

TOM. I only deal with real pilots, not sort of pilots –

> (**DOTTY** *hits him on the arm.*)

You flown before?

DOTTY. Never.

TOM. Man, we must be in trouble.

DOTTY. We'll have a few months' training.

TOM. Ah, well that's fine then. All you need. It's not that skillful. Any Tom, Dick or Harry could do it.

DOTTY. D'you think?

TOM. Clearly.

> (**DOTTY** *is a little hurt.* **TOM** *is immediately regretful.*)

DOTTY. This is why I didn't tell you. Bloody Bett.

TOM. You've such endearing names for each other.

DOTTY. Sorry. She's just so damned interfering. I didn't tell you because we only posted it today. She's already measuring herself up for the blasted uniform!

TOM. Dotty. Bett has it right, you know. You take no notice of no one, including me. I tell you, once you climb up and reach that big, beautiful blue, you will feel like you can do anything. Even touch the hand of God. So believe. Believe in you, Dotty. 'Cause no one will give you nothing in this world. This little adventure of mine has taught me that much, you know.

> *(They are very close and **DOTTY** is desperate to kiss him.)*

Do you know where they're posting you?

DOTTY. They've an all-female base down the road at Hamble. We're hoping we'll both go there.

TOM. And how will you get to Hamble? Will you amble to Hamble or...?

DOTTY. You're a fool.

> *(Beat.)*

You will write, Tom?

TOM. Of course, Dotty.

DOTTY. We must make the most of the days we have together.

> *(**TOM** rummages in his jacket pocket.)*

TOM. Here.

DOTTY. What's this?

TOM. Just a little something.

DOTTY. You did this?

TOM. Just a doodle.

DOTTY. It's a little more than a doodle, Tom. It's beautiful.

TOM. You like it?

DOTTY. I love it. It's perfect. A perfect pocket picture. I'll keep it with me. She could fly with me.

TOM. She remind me of you. Take flight, Dotty. Like the Chicki-chong.

DOTTY. Chicki...?

TOM. Chicki-chong; the little caged songbird. 'Cept I freed this one for you.

DOTTY. I love her, Tom.

> *(She's fallen for him.)*

Scene Four

(1943. A couple of weeks later. The kitchen. **DOTTY** *enters carrying a letter.)*

DOTTY. BETT! BETT! Where the bloody hell is she? Bett?!

BETT. *(Offstage.)* What?!

DOTTY. BETT!

BETT. *(Offstage.)* What?!

DOTTY. Where are you?!

BETT. *(Offstage.)* I'm on the bleedin' lav!

DOTTY. Well, can you hurry it up?!

BETT. *(Offstage.)* Not really, no!

DOTTY. Alright then, I'll come to you!

BETT. *(Offstage.)* Nooo! I'm coming! *(Entering whilst fixing herself.)* Blimey O'Reilly. What is it that can't wait for me to finish the most basic of tasks?

DOTTY. Uh. Excuse me, did you wash your hands, young lady?

BETT. Well, I thought the Germans had arrived so didn't think it necessary.

(She wipes her hand down **DOTTY***'s cheek.)*

DOTTY. You're so immature.

BETT. I do try.

So? What had to break my one moment of solitude?

DOTTY. *(Revealing the letter.)* I got in. I only bloody got in!

BETT. Oh.

DOTTY. Did you…?

BETT. I've not heard.

DOTTY. Oh. Really?

BETT. Not a dicky bird.

DOTTY. Why? I wonder why?

BETT. Too short?

DOTTY. Hmm...

BETT. Too old?

DOTTY. Oh, Bett...

> (**BETT** *smiles.*)

You're pulling my leg, aren't you?

> (**BETT** *nods.*)

You little –

BETT. I'm sorry but your face was a picture.

DOTTY. We're in. We did it.

BETT. We bloody did it!

DOTTY. We're heading for the sky...

> (*They hug.*)

Let me see then. Where's your letter?

DAD. (*Bellowing.*) BETT!

BETT. Oh god.

DAD. BETT!

BETT. I think I left it on the sideboard...

> (**DAD** *enters.*)

DAD. Bett.

DOTTY. Dad –

DAD. Dorothy, I am having this conversation with Bett, not you.

DOTTY. I know, Daddy but –

DAD. Dorothy, will you please stay out of it?

BETT. Dad.

DAD. I tell you, Elizabeth. You've done it this time.

DOTTY. *(Whispers to* **BETT** *pointedly.)* Elizabeth…

DAD. I know you think you're wise and worldly but answering this ad was perhaps the most foolish thing you have ever done.

BETT. Here we / go.

DOTTY. Daddy –

BETT. Just my luck, eh Dot?

DAD. You will need that and much more if you get up in a bloody aeroplane whilst our skies are littered with enemies waiting to shoot you down.

BETT. They are the very reason I want to get up in a bloody aeroplane –

DAD. You talk as though you'll be fighting them yourself.

BETT. I know I won't / be

DAD. You're willing to risk your life, to be a bloody delivery driver!

BETT. I know I won't be on the frontline.

DAD. You are not doing it.

BETT. I'm sorry, but I am.

DAD. You've never even stepped inside an aeroplane let alone flown one.

BETT. I know! Exciting, isn't it?

DAD. You certainly have no understanding of the power of an aircraft.

BETT. You only have yourself to blame for that.

DAD. You have not the first idea about flying.

BETT. That doesn't matter. "Ab initio", the ad said.

(Beat.)

DOTTY. Which means "From the / beginning".

DAD. Yes, yes I know what it bloody means, thank you.

DOTTY. Right-o. Good, good.

DAD. Do you realise the state that our Royal Air Force is in? Why do you think the ATA is calling on young women, like you?

BETT. To fix the mess?

DAD. Because all the healthy young men are in fighter aircrafts being shot from the sky left, right and bloody centre. You're behind the men who are missing limbs and eyes. They're bloody desperate.

BETT. Exactly, they need us –

DAD. They need *any bloody* one with a beating heart!

BETT. *("Your turn".)* Don't they, Dot?

(Beat.)

DOTTY. What?

DAD. What?

DOTTY. What?

DAD. Dot.

DOTTY. Now, Daddy don't be cross…

DAD. No, Dorothy. Please, not you.

BETT. What does he mean by that?

DOTTY. I'm sorry.

DAD. Absolutely not.

DOTTY. We can look out for each / other

DAD. No / no

DOTTY. If we both go.

DAD. What do you think this is, Dorothy? A bloody jolly?

BETT. That's what I said.

DOTTY. Whose side are you on?

DAD. It's war, Dorothy. A bloody war. Not even your brilliant imagination could conjure up what these men are facing. The sky looks very different from the seat of a war aircraft. It's like nothing you've ever known.

DOTTY. Then tell me.

DAD. You cannot begin to imagine the things that I've seen. The things I see.

DOTTY. It's not for the want of trying. We've tried, Daddy. We all tried.

DAD. You will never understand. *(To **BETT**.)* This was your idea, I take it?

BETT. I told her not to post it.

DOTTY. You two are incredible.

DAD. You are not going, Dorothy.

DOTTY. Please –

DAD. I won't allow it.

DOTTY. Please –

DAD. And that's the end of it.

DOTTY. I'm not your little girl anymore.

(Beat.)

DOTTY. Try to understand why I need to do this.

DAD. I cannot fathom for one moment.

DOTTY. Because *she* would have done it.

(Beat.)

DAD. She would

She would absolutely *not* agree to this.

> (**BETT** *and* **DOTTY** *look at* **DAD.** *They don't know what else to say.*)

If you disobey me...

(Beat.)

Please. Dorothy. Elizabeth.

> (**DAD** *looks at both of them. He is spent. He carefully folds Bett's letter back together and places it on the table and leaves.* **DOTTY** *and* **BETT** *look at each other. They hold hands as:*)

Scene Five

*(**BETT** and **DOTTY** change into their ATA uniforms. It's 1943. A few weeks later. Their training begins – this culminates in some form of take-off/flight for the sisters.)*

C.O. Welcome to the ATA. Your training will last approximately six months after which you will be based at number fifteen Ferry Pool, near Southampton. By the time you finish your training, you will be flying single-engined non-operational aeroplanes under Class One such as the Tiger Moth, Masters and Magister. Should you log enough flights and prove to be competent you may be upped to Class Two to fly aircraft such as the P51 Mustang, the Hurricane, and even the Spitfire. Ferry pilots have to navigate by means of maps and instruments and you will not have access to radio nor armament. You will fly below the clouds so avoid barrage balloons and trust to luck that you will not be shot down. Keep this with you at all times.

*(A ferry pilot book is handed to **BETT** and **DOTTY**.)*

Treat it as your Bible. This little blue book is your best friend. It holds the key to every aircraft that you will ever fly. You are civilians in uniform with military privilege and you are joining the ATA at a momentous time for women: for the first time in our history you will be paid equally to your male counterparts. Earn your place and we will reward it with the vast sky in the palm of your hands. Fly well. May blue skies always be with you.

GROUND CREW. Two thousand people replied to this ad and seventeen of you have been successful, so you must have your wits about you. You'll need them more than ever now. Our audacious leader, Pauline Gower has brought together the very finest female pilots on the planet but there is one thing that even Amy Johnson couldn't forecast. The weather here has a mind of its own and will be both your friend and foe. So listen very carefully to the following. This is your training aircraft; the de Haviland Tiger Moth. Please, step inside the cockpit.

INSTRUCTOR. You will see six gauges in front of you. Turn and slip, airspeed indicator, RPM Gauge, altimeter, compass and clock. The compass and clock are the most important for navigation. The altimeter records the height of the machine and should be set to zero on the ground. Fly no higher than two thousand feet and never below eight hundred feet. First off, let's get fuel to the cylinders. Open the fuel valve now. Make sure the ignition is off. Your ground crew will prime the engine and turn the prop to suck the fuel into the system, ready to ignite. Now, pull your stick back and set your throttle about a half-inch open. The magneto switches are up to your left. Up for on, down for off. Turn it up. Now.

BETT & DOTTY. Contact.

INSTRUCTOR. Take hold of the stick in your right hand and using your feet on the rudder pedals, taxi into the wind. Now, get ready to take off. At forty miles per hour ease the stick back and the aeroplane will start to fly.

This is it, cadets.

You're moments away from touching the big blue.

Enjoy the bumpy ride.

Chocks away!

Scene Six

(Hamble Ferry Pool. Winter 1943. The weather is terrible. The ATA motto "Aetheris Avidi" hangs above them – "Eager for the Air" and a sign saying, "We pay you to be safe, not brave".)

*(**DOTTY** is doing a balancing exercise, pretending to be an aeroplane. **BETT** is counting the time on her wristwatch whilst **JOY**, another ATA Pilot, makes a pot of tea. **JIMMY**, from the ground crew, reads the paper, smoking. At last, **DOTTY** loses her balance and falls to the floor in a heap.)*

JOY. Ah what?! How long was that?

BETT. Worse than the last time.

DOTTY. Alright, alright. You do it then, smart Alec.

BETT. With pleasure.

JIMMY. Why can't you lot just sit down and read a book?

JOY. We've gotta keep on form, Jim. Ooh, can I pinch a ciggy?

JIMMY. Do you know there's a war on?

JOY. Rationing doesn't come into it when you pilfer them from the engineer's shed.

> *(**JIMMY** reluctantly hands one to **JOY** who takes the pack.)*

Ta. Want one, Dot?

JIMMY. Oh for Pete's sake.

DOTTY. Thanks.

> *(**JOY** puts one behind her ear.)*

JOY. Bett?

BETT. Oooh, ta, Joy.

> (**JOY** *hands another to* **BETT**.)

JIMMY. Oh come on...

JOY. Right. Back to the job at hand.

BETT. It's all in the mind, you know.

JOY. *(Lighting a ciggy.)* I'm sure.

DOTTY. And the balancing. A little in the balancing.

> (**BETT** *takes the position of an aeroplane, balancing on one leg, as* **JOY** *lights* **DOTTY**'s *cigarette.*)

Ta.

JIMMY. How long does she have to hold it for?

JOY. Until she falls.

DOTTY. She'll be ages, we may as well brew up.

JIMMY. I'll be mother.

JOY. I made a pot just now.

DOTTY. Not too strong for me, please.

BETT. Can I have mine without the saucer?

> *(They look at her and smile.)*

DOTTY. Remember when we played "chicken" on the cattle grid at the end of our lane?

BETT. Oh, you love bringing this up.

DOTTY. Because it's so funny.

BETT. Is it? Is it though?

DOTTY. Yes. We'd spent, what, about fifteen minutes trying to push each other off and just as we declared it a draw, she moved to walk off and fell down the bloody thing!

BETT. Past my knee.

JOY. Ouch!

DOTTY. Mum had to rub spit all over her leg to loosen it out.

JIMMY. Urgh.

BETT. Just as a stampede of Jersey cows made a beeline for me.

*(They all laugh except **JIMMY**.)*

JIMMY. Oh, that is my worst nightmare.

JOY. What? Being trapped?

JIMMY. No. Jersey cows.

(Beat.)

DOTTY. Which leg was it? This one *(She tickles her.)* Or this one? *(She tickles her.)*

BETT. I won't be bullied!

DOTTY. One of your knees is much fatter than the other though, isn't it? Is it this one? *(She tickles her.)*

BETT. It's all in the mind. It's all in the mind.

*(**JIMMY** brings the tea.)*

JOY. Oooh, thanks, Jimbo.

JIMMY. Here you are, ladies.

DOTTY. I'll take Bett's.

*(**DOTTY** holds it out to **BETT** but it's too far from her reach.)*

BETT. Dotty.

DOTTY. Your arms are much shorter than I thought.

BETT. Shut up.

DOTTY. How do you reach the controls?

BETT. Just give it to me.

DOTTY. Here you are.

BETT. You keep moving it further away!

DOTTY. You're so close.

BETT. This is sabotage.

DOTTY. It's on your fingertips.

BETT. Just bring it closer.

DOTTY. Alright, alright.

(She moves to another angle.)

Better?

BETT. No!

*(**BETT** stretches and falls. They all feign disappointment.)*

JOY. You nearly split your difference there, pet.

BETT. She's an utter juvenile.

DOTTY. I'm not the one pretending to be an aeroplane.

JOY. Touché.

BETT. How long did I manage?

JOY. Ah, I didn't... Did either of you...?

*(**DOTTY** and **JIMMY** shake their heads.)*

BETT. You're joking!

DOTTY. It's not the winning, Betty…

BETT. It absolutely is.

DOTTY. Here you are. You must be parched, old thing.

> (**DOTTY** *hands* **BETT** *her cup of tea and kisses her on the cheek.*)

BETT. It's a ruddy fix.

> (*They all drink and* **BETT** *lights her cigarette.*)

DOTTY. Is it letting up at all out there?

JIMMY. Not really, it's scrub for the day. They'll be stacking up nicely for you.

JOY. Oh deary, we'll have a busy few days ahead of us if the sky keeps leaking, girlies. 'Cause you won't get me up in this, that's for sure.

BETT. Who makes that call then?

DOTTY. We do, surely?

JOY. Ah, no, well. Us girls all tend to follow suit but that's where it all gets a little hazy.

JIMMY. That's one way to put it!

JOY. It's a rock and a hard place; they need the aircraft delivered, but they can't afford to lose pilots doing it.

JIMMY. They need more pilots then.

JOY. Not as simple as that though, is it?

JIMMY. They could train more.

JOY. Could they?

JIMMY. Of course. There's plenty of people wanting to do their bit.

JOY. Pop in and offer your services then, if we're all so disposable.

JIMMY. Oh, I'm not saying –

JOY. Oh, not you. You're not suggesting yourself.

JIMMY. I can't fly an aeroplane. I can barely mount a pushbike.

JOY. Don't you want to do your bit?

JIMMY. I'm doing my bit; supporting you lot from the ground. Look, all I'm saying is they could do with a bit more manpower.

(They all squint.)

BETT. Oh dear.

JOY. Careful, there's a 'ruddy great hole right behind you, Jimbo.

DOTTY. Do you want me to fetch a spade for you?

JIMMY. Womanpower. I mean womanpower. Any power. They need more power from the sex. Sex. Not sex. Sex. Gender. Man or Woman. Wherever they can get it.

The power. Not the sex.

*(**JIMMY**'s exhausted. **BETT** and **DOTTY** are sniggering.)*

JOY. But the thing is, Jim boy, no amount of sex can control that out there…

JIMMY. Eh?

*(**DOTTY** and **BETT** are beside themselves.)*

JOY. *(Gesturing the weather.)* We're at the mercy of old Nimbus. 'Specially here in Hamble. You know, I think it's actually brightening up.

DOTTY, JIMMY & BETT. Thank God.

JOY. Just as we're having our tea.

JIMMY. Take it up with you.

DOTTY. Can we?

JIMMY. Yes, of course.

JOY. Don't listen to him, he's yanking your stick.

| **BETT.** | **DOTTY.** |
| Haha | Oh very good. |

JOY. I'm off to the little girls' room before they send us all up.

BETT. I'll come with. Not the place to be caught short.

JOY. It's not ideal.

JIMMY. That's why you should take your teacup.

ALL. Oh, Jimmy / Oh no. For heaven's sake.

JOY. Ta, ta all.

BETT. Blue Skies, Dotty.

DOTTY. Blue Skies.

(**BETT** and **JOY** exit.)

JIMMY. I best get on myself. Think I've outstayed my welcome.

DOTTY. Oh no, Jimmy, we love our little chats with you. Hopefully see you at the pub later.

JIMMY. Smashin'. We've tuned the piano at long last, so you'll hear the racket before you land, no doubt.

DOTTY. Excellent – I'll warm up on the descent.

(**DOTTY** sings a chromatic scale down.)

JIMMY. You're wasted here, Dot.

(Gulps his tea down and picks up his paper.)

Blue Skies.

(**JIMMY** *exits.*)

DOTTY. Blue Skies, Jimmy.

(The sound of the Spitfire comes in. **DOTTY** *slowly stands on one leg and balances like an aeroplane. This transitions into a moment of flight for* **DOTTY**.*)*

Scene Seven

(February 1944. Evening. The Ferry Pool at Hamble.)

DOTTY. Oh Bett! Betty, Bett, Bett.

It was incredible…

It was –

I've never known anything like it.

The power of the thing.

It felt like someone had booted me up the

It makes the Tiger Moth feel like a pig.

Honestly

I'm the luckiest girl alive!

I was a little nervous, I have to admit but

Flying…

F l y i n g.

Just you and the blue.

It's almost like flying yourself.

Like they'd sewn wings on my back.

How a bird feels.

I felt like I could breathe on the controls and it would answer me.

It's built for us, isn't it?

Built for Women. Everything in the right place.

Heaven. Utter heaven.

(Pause.)

I heard you broke a Mosquito yesterday.

BETT. I didn't break it –

DOTTY. No, no of course you didn't.

BETT. I didn't break it.

DOTTY. No, no.

BETT. Not completely.

DOTTY. I'm sure they can still use it for ice cream deliveries or –

BETT. It was just a tyre. They can fix a bloody tyre.

DOTTY. The Spitfire. I've flown The Spit. I can't believe it!

BETT. It won't be the last time.

DOTTY. I hope not.

(She lights a cigarette.)

Everyone out on a chit, are they?

BETT. Must be. I've only just got back myself.

DOTTY. What did you have?

BETT. Why? Are you keeping a log for me?

DOTTY. Just interested, Bett.

BETT. I took a Hurricane to Eastleigh this morning, then an Oxford to Cranfield and the Anson back. Don't you need to jot all this down…?

DOTTY. What's the matter?

(Beat.)

Is it because I flew the Spit?

BETT. Why would that…?

DOTTY. I can only fly what they give me, Bett.

BETT. I know, but you could take a bit more…

DOTTY. What?

> *(Beat.)*

Right-o. Will you come tonight?

BETT. –

DOTTY. I'll look after you. Promise.

BETT. I don't think I –

DOTTY. You can leave when you've had enough.

BETT. I don't really feel like it.

> *(**DOTTY** smiles at her.)*

DOTTY. If you're sure. I'll head on, then.

BETT. Alright, Dot.

> *(Beat.)*

DOTTY. Do you get scared?

BETT. What?

DOTTY. Up there.

BETT. No. It's the one place I feel... Why? Do you?

DOTTY. No. But when I was up there today. It's

Lonely.

In a way

Don't you think?

It's

We're free but

I don't know.

Makes you think about things. Plenty of time to do that, isn't there? When we're not trying to find the hedges and dodge the Jerrys.

DOTTY. And I worry

I worry

About you.

If you're

If you're happy.

Bett.?

Are you?

Are you happy?

> *(They look at each other.)*

I –

BETT. I'm alright, Dot.

> *(They smile.)*

DOTTY. Did you hear what Mary took out yesterday?

BETT. The Wellington? I know...

DOTTY. Bloody great thing. I hope I don't get one of those. They didn't believe her, you know.

BETT. Who?

DOTTY. The ground crew.

BETT. What?

DOTTY. When she landed. They didn't believe she flew / it.

BETT. Eh?

DOTTY. She said she got out. And they all climbed in. In the bomber. All the men. And they were looking.

BETT. Oh?

DOTTY. Searching

BETT. For what?

DOTTY. For the pilot. For The Man!

BETT. Good lord.

DOTTY. I suppose they thought her tiny, tiny hands couldn't quite reach the controls. Won't ever change, will it? The men will always be searching the cockpits for, well…

BETT. Dot!

DOTTY. What?

BETT. You're very naughty.

>   *(Beat.)*

DOTTY. *(Looking at wristwatch.)* I best get to the pub. The girls'll think I've been shot down.

BETT. Of course. Go.

DOTTY. You sure you…?

BETT. I'm sure.

DOTTY. Joy's showing off her new fella.

>   *(***BETT** *shakes her head.)*

Alright. See you.

>   *(***DOTTY** *exits.* **BETT** *looks after her. She stands. Frozen. We see her fears for Dotty grow as the C.O's Office is built around her.)*

Scene Eight

(The next day; February 1944. The Commanding Officer's office. **BETT** *enters to find the* **COMMANDER** *consumed with paperwork.)*

C.O. Good morning. Please. Sit.

BETT. Thank you, Commander.

C.O. What can I do you for?

BETT. Thank you for seeing me, Commander.

C.O. Of course.

BETT. This. This is not easy for me.

C.O. Go on.

BETT. It's

I

So

The thing is

(Beat.)

C.O. Third Officer Finlay... *(Gesturing the time.)*

BETT. Yes

Right

Alright

I feel

It's my duty

And my responsibility

On various levels –

C.O. Bett, I know this may be hard for you but please be direct and spit the bloody words out.

BETT. I'm worried, Commander. I'm worried about Third Officer Finlay. And I'm not talking in the third person.

C.O. Your sister.

BETT. Yes, Commander. She recently went out on a chit in very bad weather –

C.O. Yes, I am aware of / this.

BETT. Very bad weather.

C.O. And I will talk to her in due course.

BETT. Right.

It's just

You see

It's not the first time.

And I wouldn't put it past her doing it again and again.

C.O. Well, we can't predict the future, can we?

BETT. No.

C.O. So let's deal with the present, shall we?

BETT. I don't think she appreciates the risks –

C.O. You both joined the ATA at the same time, with the same experience (or lack thereof) and underwent the same training. So, you are both equipped with equal knowledge and understanding. Why is she at more risk than you?

BETT. Because she's foolhardy! She's bloody-minded. She's –

C.O. Your little sister?

(Beat.)

C.O. We all knew your situation had the potential to be tricky, shall we say? We appreciate your desire to be posted to the same ferry pool which was always going to pose difficulties. But in this building and in that sky, she is not your sister. She is your comrade, your colleague. And when one is in an aircraft one is on one's own and one must make one's own decisions. That is the pilot's responsibility. That is Dot's responsibility.

BETT. Of course.

C.O. I will talk to her.

BETT. Thank you, Commander.

C.O. Now, I must get on.

BETT. Yes. Thank you. Commander? I trust this conversation is in confidence?

C.O. It is.

BETT. Thank you.

> (**BETT** *moves to the door.*)

C.O. You can't protect her when she's up there, you know.

BETT. I know.

> (*Beat.*)

C.O. Very good.

> (**BETT** *leaves as the sound of aircraft increases.*)

Scene Nine

(The Ferry Pool. February 1944. A few days later. **BETT** *and* **DOTTY** *are listening to the radio.)*

(They smoke.)

A broadcast plays the following from Stafford Cripps:[*]

"The People of this country should know and understand the contribution that the ATA has made and is making to our war effort. Your record of deliveries of aircraft is now well past the one hundred thousand mark and the mileage flown exceeds thirty million miles, which indicates, I think, the very great extent of your work. Then too ,there is the remarkable fact that neither age nor sex disqualifies people from becoming pilots... I cannot but turn my mind for a moment to those who no longer fill your ranks, those who have in your service given their lives; isolated and alone in various parts of our country...we give honour and grateful remembrance –

DOTTY. Alright, Crippsy that's enough, I thank you!

(She turns it off.)

BETT. Oi!

DOTTY. We don't need to hear all that.

BETT. Don't we?

DOTTY. *Do* we?

*(***BETT** *shrugs.)*

---

[*] A licence to produce *Spitfire Girls* does not include a performance licence for any third-party or copyrighted recordings. Licensees should create their own.

DOTTY. I've got to get up there in five minutes so I'd rather not be reminded of the many, many dangers, thank you very much.

BETT. *(Sotto.)* Perhaps you should be.

> *(Beat.)*

DOTTY. Sorry?

BETT. Nothing.

> *(Beat.)*

DOTTY. You'll come tonight?

BETT. ?

DOTTY. To the pub. The girls are giddy to meet Tom.

BETT. Ah yes.

> *(Beat.)*

DOTTY. I'd really like you to come.

BETT. I'll see.

DOTTY. Right.

> *(Sound of chatter and doors closing and opening.)*

(Getting ready.) Sounds like Operations are opening up. I wonder what's on the menu today. "For starters, I'll have The Swordfish, followed by a Hurricane then the Barracuda – no, no – a Spitfire for pudding, please".

> *(**BETT** smiles as they gather up their bits.)*

It's looking like good flying out there today. Fingers crossed, we'll be home for tea…and Tom.

BETT. Tea and Tom. Yes.

> *(Beat.)*

DOTTY. What *did* you mean.?

> (**BETT** *looks.*)

Just now, after I cut Cripps short.

BETT. Nothing.

DOTTY. Look, have I done something?

BETT. No, no.

DOTTY. No?

BETT. It's nothing, Dot.

> (**DOTTY** *smiles.*)

What?

DOTTY. Doesn't matter.

BETT. What?

DOTTY. It's just – I've been trying, Bett. But it's just the usual… *(Gestures nothing.)*

BETT. That's not fair.

DOTTY. I know it's not. But I can't read your mind, Betty. I thought this adventure of ours would bring us closer together.

BETT. We are close, Dot.

DOTTY. We are

But

You need / to

BETT. What? What do I need to do?

> *(Beat.)*

I'm sorry.

DOTTY. I just wish I could help / you.

BETT. I'm alright, Dotty.

> *(Beat.)*

I am.

DOTTY. I will always be here, Bett.

> *(A tender moment and then **TOM** enters.)*

TOM. Where is she?

DOTTY. Tom!

TOM. Dotty, Dotty, Dotty.

> *(**TOM** picks up **DOTTY** in a cliché embrace.)*

DOTTY. You're early. What are you doing here? *(To **TOM**.)* You shouldn't be here.

*(To **BETT**.)* He shouldn't be here.

BETT. You shouldn't be here.

TOM. Ah, they don't mind. It's a thrill for them to have a real pilot on the premises.

> *(**DOTTY** whacks him on the arm.)*

Hey!

DOTTY. I want to stay, Tom, but I need to pick up my chit next door.

TOM. Pick up your what now…?

DOTTY. Chit.

BETT. *(Spelling it out.)* C.H.I.T.

TOM. Ohhh… I thought you said sh–

DOTTY. It's our itinerary for the day

TOM. I see…

DOTTY. It's the best part. Finding out what we have.

TOM. I wish I could come up with you.

BETT. You can't.

DOTTY. You can't, Tom. I wish you could. But I'll see you as soon as I've landed.

TOM. I'll be waiting, Dotty.

BETT. We should go.

DOTTY. I'm sorry I have to rush off.

BETT. You'll see each other in a few hours. Come on Dot. We'll be late and we're never late.

DOTTY. I'll be right there.

> (**BETT** *shakes her head and leaves.* **DOTTY** *moves close to* **TOM**.)

TOM. Go.

DOTTY. I'll be counting down the minutes.

TOM. Me too.

DOTTY. I've missed you so much, Tom.

TOM. Same here, Dotty.

DOTTY. There were times when I thought I might never see you again. Did you get my last letter?

TOM. Uh-huh.

DOTTY. Why didn't you...?

> *(Beat.)*

I thought something...

TOM. It's another world in those fighters. It chips away at all your good bits. You're my shining light in all this mess, you know.

> *(She holds him.)*

TOM. Go.

DOTTY. I don't want to.

TOM. Go. Don't tarnish your impeccable record because of me.

DOTTY. I don't care about that.

TOM. You do. You swot.

> *(He straightens her tie, then holds her face ever so gently, she kisses him. They lose themselves in each other's eyes.)*

Blue skies, Dotty.

> *(**DOTTY** walks to the door, smiles back at him and leaves. **TOM** recalibrates. Takes out his sketchbook and begins to draw. After a moment, **BETT** enters.)*

Dotty...

BETT. Forgot my bag.

TOM. Ah.

> *(**BETT** picks up her bag.)*

See you later?

BETT. Maybe.

TOM. You alright?

BETT. Fine and dandy.

> *(Beat.)*

When do you go back?

TOM. Tomorrow. Air support in the Netherlands.

BETT. How is it?

TOM. It's the darkest place on earth. I wouldn't send my worst enemy there.

(He gives a wry smile.)

BETT. You look...

TOM. I know, Betty. I am an old man now. We all are.

(Beat.)

I'm going to propose.

BETT. To Dot?

TOM. Of course. To Dotty.

BETT. Good. I'm happy for you.

TOM. You are?

BETT. Yes. You're a good man, Tom. You try very hard not to be but you are.

(A moment.)

If, however, you do anything to hurt her I will strap you to the wing of a bomber in your underpants and drop you at Hitler's doorstep.

TOM. That's a joke, right?

BETT. Only if you laugh.

*(**TOM** just about manages a smile for her.)*

Congratulations.

*(They smile at each other. **TOM** takes out a picture from his pocket and hands it to **BETT**.)*

Tom, I...

TOM. For a friend. Just a friend.

(Beat.)

BETT. Thank you. It's beautiful.

> (**BETT** *smiles, folds the paper puts it in her pocket and leaves.* **TOM** *turns back to his sketchbook.)*

Scene Ten

(Hamble Ferry Pool. February 1944. The next day. **DOTTY** *pours herself a cup of tea.* **BETT** *enters.)*

BETT. Morning.

DOTTY. Morning.

BETT. Sore head?

(Beat.)

Turned out to be quite the engagement party, didn't it?

(Beat.)

Enough for another?

*(***DOTTY** *puts the pot down.)*

Everything alright?

DOTTY. Fine.

BETT. Right.

(Pause.)

DOTTY. So the Commander has asked to see me.

BETT. Oh?

DOTTY. Yes. And it seems serious.

(Beat.)

Any ideas what that might be?

*(***BETT** *is still.)*

You spoke to her about me, didn't you?

BETT. How did you...?

DOTTY. The girls told me last night they saw you leaving her office the other day, and, well, your face has just confirmed it.

BETT. Look –

DOTTY. You've been especially off with me for ages and I couldn't quite put my finger on it.

BETT. Dotty –

DOTTY. I fully expect to get a rocket from her. But I didn't think my own sister would go behind my back.

BETT. It wasn't like that, Dot.

DOTTY. Right.

BETT. I was simply looking out for you.

DOTTY. Don't you see how it undermines me?

BETT. I didn't / mean

DOTTY. Big sister looking after baby.

BETT. I know.

DOTTY. I secured my place here on my own merit.

BETT. I know.

DOTTY. Just as you did.

BETT. I know.

DOTTY. I have never once questioned your capability or your right to be / here.

BETT. No.

DOTTY. So why did you do it?

BETT. I'm just trying to protect you.

DOTTY. I don't need protection, Bett.

BETT. Look, maybe we should talk about this when we're both feeling a little / brighter.

DOTTY. Actually, I'd like to talk about it now.

BETT. Well I don't.

DOTTY. Well, you never do.

BETT. Oh here we go again.

DOTTY. No, no.

BETT. Don't bring it round to me.

DOTTY. You never talk to me, Bett. You never talk to me, however hard I try but somehow you plucked up the courage to talk to the C.O. About me.

BETT. I went to the Commander because you put yourself and others, I may add, at risk that day.

DOTTY. Why don't you talk to me, Bett?

BETT. You should have stayed on the ground. You shouldn't have flown.

DOTTY. Why don't you talk to me?

BETT. No one else did.

DOTTY. Why don't you talk to me?

BETT. You're a fine pilot but you're bloody foolish.

DOTTY. Why don't you talk to me?

BETT. Because I don't know what to say!

(Beat.)

DOTTY. If only I was the C.O.

(Pause.)

BETT. I only have one sister. When she decides to take to the air on one of the most hazardous bloody days in living memory, I feel the need to protect her from repeating the incident and killing herself. That's why I went to our Commander. That's why I would do it again.

(Beat.)

DOTTY. You're jealous.

BETT. What?

DOTTY. You can't bear that it comes naturally to me.

BETT. No, Dot. That's not / what

DOTTY. It's easy for me.

BETT. That's not what this is about.

DOTTY. Why did you do it then?

BETT. For the reasons I've just said.

DOTTY. I'm not the first one to have flown in bad weather. That notice is being broken all the time. I landed safely and delivered the aircraft in one piece. What's the problem?

BETT. You shouldn't have flown.

DOTTY. Stop telling me what to do!

(Beat.)

BETT. I'm not trying to hurt you, Dot.

DOTTY. Right.

BETT. It's the truth.

DOTTY. But you have, Bett. You really bloody have.

*(**DOTTY** moves to the door.)*

BETT. Please, Dot. Dot!

*(**DOTTY** leaves.)*

Scene Eleven

(A couple of days later; in February 1944. The Commander's Office. The **COMMANDER** *is on the phone as* **DOTTY** *enters.)*

C.O. Yes. Yes, to come directly to my office. And no need to knock. Thank you.

(She hangs up.) Please, sit down, Third Officer Finlay.

DOTTY. Thank you, Commander.

(She sits.)

I know why you want to see me and I just want to say that what I did last week was dangerous –

C.O. It was.

DOTTY. I know. And foolish and reckless and I will never do it again.

C.O. I hope not.

DOTTY. I'm due to log my flights with you soon and I hope you will consider me for new / aircraft.

C.O. Of course. Would you please sit down?

DOTTY. Yes.

(She sits. **C.O.** *paces.)*

Commander, I have a clean record of deliveries –

C.O. I know that.

DOTTY. I know I'm not as experienced as many others but I'm really good at what I / do.

C.O. Dot, I know all this.

DOTTY. *(Standing.)* Please, this place is the best thing that has ever happened to me, I don't want to lose it.

C.O. I understand.

DOTTY. Bett had every right to come and express her concerns to you but it was a bit bloody – excuse my French – a bit off, to say the least.

C.O. Dot, I've not called you in here to discuss your sister.

DOTTY. I know but (being a Virgo) she does have a tendency to stick her nose in where it's not bloody wanted.

C.O. Third Officer!

DOTTY. Sorry.

C.O. I need you to listen.

DOTTY. Sorry. I am. I've got it off my chest now. All better.

C.O. Good. Please can you sit down?

DOTTY. Of course. *(She sits.)*

> *(Beat.)*

C.O. I've just received a telephone call…

DOTTY. Right.

C.O. I regret to inform you… There's been an accident.

DOTTY. Accident?

C.O. Yes.

DOTTY. Right.

C.O. Just this morning.

DOTTY. Right.

C.O. They tell me there's no question of who it is.

DOTTY. Who what is?

C.O. Naturally, they wanted to get the message to you as quickly as possible.

(Beat.)

I'm sorry to be the one to tell you.

(Beat.)

Flight Sergeant Lawley.

(Pause.)

DOTTY. I'm supposed to be on a job. Sorry. Can we do this...

C.O. He would have been killed instantly.

DOTTY. What?

What are you...?

Sorry

I think you must be...

Did I bring my bag in?

I thought I put it down...

What did you just say?

> *(**C.O.** pours a drink and looks towards the door. She puts it on the table in front of **DOTTY**.)*

C.O. Here. Drink this.

> *(**BETT** enters. **DOTTY** stares.)*

Dot, have you understood what I've just said? Thomas Lawley's fighter was shot down over Nijmegen this morning.

BETT. *(Punctured.)* What?

C.O. His squadron lost a number of men.

BETT. Tom?

DOTTY. But...

BETT. *(Sotto.)* Oh God.

DOTTY. But he can't be.

We were just

We were...

He was just here...he was just.

*(**BETT** moves to **DOTTY**.)*

BETT. Dot. Dotty.

DOTTY. Bett. They're telling me he's

But he can't bec–

because we just got –

didn't we?

He asked me to marry

I mean he can't –

and then

*(**BETT** moves to **DOTTY**.)*

BETT. He's gone, Dotty.

DOTTY. No.

BETT. Tom's gone.

DOTTY. No.

BETT. I'm so sorry.

DOTTY. No.

BETT. I'm so sorry.

DOTTY. No. No.

No, no, no, no, no, no, no, no, no, no, NO!

He was just here.

He was just –

> (**BETT** *holds* **DOTTY** *for dear life as her sobs echo around the Commander's office.*)

Interval

ACT TWO

Scene One

("Blue Skies" plays. **DOTTY** and **TOM** enter. They look as youthful, radiant and joyful as they ever have. They edge towards each other like Fred & Ginger and dance. It's tender and beautiful.)*

*(The **BETT** of 1960 watches them from a distance. The world of **DOTTY** and **TOM** gradually dissolves until we realise we are in...)*

---

* A licence to produce *Spitfire Girls* does not include a performance licence for any third-party or copyrighted recordings. Licensees should create their own.

Scene Two

(The pub – early hours of 1960. It's New Year's Day. And it's still raining. We're just on the other side of closing. **BETT**, *with a mop in hand, is lost in thought as* **FRANK** *watches her. He smokes a pipe.)*

FRANK. Penny for 'em?

BETT. Good grief, Frank. Thought you'd gone.

FRANK. Nope.

BETT. *(Quietly.)* Wishful thinking.

FRANK. Eh?

BETT. Nothing.

FRANK. Penny for your thoughts?

BETT. *(Smiling.)* Not enough pennies in the world, Frank.

FRANK. Try me.

BETT. You'd be broke in no time.

FRANK. Already am.

*(**BETT** thinks for a moment but –)*

BETT. I must get on with all this. *(Gestures pint.)* Wanna get on with that?

FRANK. Right-o, love.

BETT. Don't forget to take them on with you.

FRANK. What's that?

BETT. The shoes, Frank. The shoes.

FRANK. Oh, right-o. Thanks, love.

BETT. He better be wearing them next time I see him.

FRANK. He will.

BETT. Because if they disappear like the last pair –

FRANK. They won't.

BETT. Right you are, Frank.

(*As he gathers his bits together.*)

FRANK. Happy New Year my dear an' keep that there chin up.

BETT. I will.

FRANK. No, no. You must keep your chin up, else it pulls your soul down, my dear.

BETT. Uh-huh. Right.

FRANK. We all know, Bett. You've been through the wars in more than one / way.

BETT. Na-night Frank...

FRANK. We know that. But you're a grand girl. I know I've had a few milds but you need to take care of yourself.

BETT. I do.

FRANK. If the last twenty year has taught me anything, it's to grab life by its scruffy neck and pull with all your soddin' strength.

BETT. I'm just getting the bucket –

(**BETT** *leaves.*)

FRANK. Otherwise. Otherwise life, Bett. Life will spit you out and ol' Dorothy will come along and 'elp 'erself to it. Where she to, anyways? I miss my four-legged friend lying next to me here.

(**BETT** *returns with a mop and bucket.*)

BETT. You want to finish this up now, love?

(**FRANK** *downs half of his pint. No problem.*)

FRANK. Yertizz. And it caint be any tizzer.

> (**BETT** *shakes her head, smiling as she takes the glass.*)

You don't 'alf look after your beer. Bloody lovely pint of mild, that.

BETT. Clean pipes. That's the trick.

FRANK. If you looked after yourself as much as your beer you'd be...

BETT. What Frank?

FRANK. You'd be... You'd be one "ale" of a girl.

BETT. Brilliant.

FRANK. Well, I can't stand around here gassin', Bett. I've gotta get back to Jack.

BETT. Is he on his own then?

FRANK. Yeh, yeh.

BETT. Where's Barb?

FRANK. She had to see to her friend, so I said I'd have the lad.

BETT. But you've not got him, Frank.

FRANK. He's alright, he's a bright kid –

BETT. Bloody hell...

FRANK. He's alright.

BETT. Get back home will you?

FRANK. Alright, alright. Don't fret, Bett. *(He laughs.)* Don't. Fret. Bett.

BETT. Good God, Frank. He's five years old.

FRANK. He knows where I be, if he needs me. 'Tis only a hundred yards down the road.

BETT. Get back to your little boy.

FRANK. Right-o, Bett. Cheero, then.

> (**BETT** *shakes her head.* **FRANK** *finally leaves.*)

BETT. Unbelievable.

> (**BETT** *lights a cigarette and continues to mop.* **DOTTY** *enters. She sees the shoes on the bar.*)

DOTTY. Unlucky that.

BETT. What is?

DOTTY. Shoes on the bar.

BETT. Oh God.

DOTTY. Well, I suppose it's a table, really / but

BETT. He's useless.

DOTTY. And only if they're new.

BETT. He'll be back first thing anyway.

DOTTY. They don't look new.

BETT. They're not new.

> (*Beat.*)

Where have you been?

DOTTY. (*Gesturing to the* Picture Post *on the bar.*) Oh look, she was beautiful, wasn't she?

BETT. Oh yes, I dug it out earlier. I knew I kept a copy. Found it amongst the sheet music through there.

DOTTY. She was a great cover girl for us, eh?

BETT. Mmm.

DOTTY. You could have done an equally good job of it, I reckon.

BETT. Yes?

(She recreates the look.)

DOTTY. Maybe not.

*(**BETT** swings the mop at her.)*

Good to see you know your place now though. Mop in hand. No more silly ideas about being a pilot.

BETT. Oh, I know my rank, Sir. Back where I should be. Mopping up the spit rather than flying it.

DOTTY. What year was that?

BETT. Umm, I don't know. Oh, hang on… 1944, it says.

(They look at each other.)

I never knew what to say.

DOTTY. Nothing would have helped, Bett. He was the love of my entire life. All we had to do was get through the war without falling from the sky. And he fell from the sky. After he promised his life to me. Nothing would have helped. Nothing.

BETT. I should have said more. I could have helped you if only I opened my stupid mouth for once.

DOTTY. It's not your fault.

BETT. Perhaps –

DOTTY. It's not your fault. He died and it took the wind out of me.

(Pause.)

Can I ask you something?

BETT. Of course.

DOTTY. Did Tom love you?

BETT. What? No.

DOTTY. Because I know he gave you that picture.

    *(**BETT** looks at **DOTTY**.)*

BETT. Look. When you first started courting…we were all sort of pals together, weren't we? We all hit it off.

DOTTY. Did we? I always thought you hated him.

BETT. I

    I didn't…

    He was just

    He gave me that picture –

DOTTY. When?

BETT. What?

DOTTY. When? When did he give it to you?

BETT. I

    I can't re–

DOTTY. – remember?

    (Beat.)

BETT. I

    I don't know why I kept it. I suppose I saw in it a certain hope? Silly, really.

DOTTY. He gave me one too. Seems they were ten a penny.

BETT. No, Dot. He was mad for you.

DOTTY. Did you love him?

    *(**BETT** looks at **DOTTY**.)*

BETT. He loved you. He really loved you. Only you.

(**DAD** *enters. He picks up the* Picture Post *from the bar. The sound of aircraft slowly coming in.*)

DOTTY. I suppose so. Doesn't matter now, does it? That's all in the past. What did Dad used to say? "What's done is done and cannot be undone."

BETT. Huh. Not heard that in a good while. I never understood what he meant.

DOTTY. Mmmnn. 'Twas one of his more sombre catchphrases for us.

BETT. *(Half laughing.)* It couldn't have been easy for him. A house full of women.

DOTTY. Didn't help himself, though, did he?

BETT. Could you ever forgive him?

DOTTY. I don't know. I don't know.

(**DAD** *moves to:*)

Scene Three

(The C.O.'s office. April 1944. **DAD** *stands awkwardly, clasping the* Picture Post.*)*

C.O. Please, sit down.

DAD. Thank you. I'd rather stand.

C.O. Right you are. If you're happy to wait for the girls before / we

DAD. Actually, I wanted to talk to you without them in earshot.

C.O. Fire away.

DAD. I will come straight to the point. I need them back on the farm.

C.O. Right.

DAD. I know they are...serving their... I know you need them here doing their bit. But my need, I have to say, is greater than yours. Greater than the ATA's.

C.O. That is debatable. There is a war on and they're fulfilling a role that we cannot do without.

DAD. They were fulfilling a role on the farm that I have been living without for the best part of a year.

C.O. I appreciate that but there are labourers, are there not, that you can employ for those duties?

DAD. And how do you propose I pay them, Madam?

C.O. Well that, sir, is not my concern.

DAD. It is. Because you have stolen my workforce.

C.O. Third Officers Bett and Dot Finlay are fast becoming my most valued ferry pilots and I am not prepared to let them go. You, of all people, should be aware of what they are doing.

DAD. With all due respect, Madam, they are not on the frontline.

C.O. That doesn't lessen their value.

DAD. No, but please don't compare –

C.O. Your daughters may not be fighter pilots but what they are doing should be recognised as being equally valuable. I respect and admire your endeavours during the last / war

DAD. I merely photographed enemy ground. I don't claim to be a hero and I ask that my daughters do not do so either.

(Knock at the door.)

C.O. Come in.

*(**BETT** and **DOTTY** enter.)*

BETT. Commander.

DOTTY. Commander.

C.O. Your father wishes to speak with you directly.

BETT. Dad.

DOTTY. You came!

BETT. How are you?

DAD. Fine, fine. Time is against us, so I'll be brief. I've already been over this with your…um…

C.O. Commanding Officer.

DAD. Yes. Right. Commanding Officer. I've already been through this with your Commanding Officer and I would very much like to get this over with and get back to work. So. I need you, both of you, to give this up and return to the farm. To your home.

*(**BETT** and **DOTTY** stare.)*

Immediately.

(Pause.)

DOTTY. I –

BETT. Dad –

DAD. No, I don't want to discuss it. I'm telling you to come home.

(Beat.)

I've let you have your go but I'm doing the job of five men with those bloody pigs. I need you to come back and fulfill your responsibilities to the family.

DOTTY. Are you not going to ask how we are? How I am?

DAD. I can see how you are. I've seen it all in this! *(Holding up the* Picture Post.*)* This seems to be a very different war from the one that I was looking down on. The photographs I took certainly didn't end up in *Vogue* and *Tatler*.

DOTTY. I can't do this. Commander, can I be dismissed?

DAD. No you bloody can't. I am your father and you will offer me the respect and time that I deserve.

DOTTY. Why? Why should I? You storm in here with your usual bluff and bluster, taken in by the tripe in the papers. My Tom died. He died in the sky; in the shadows of your friends. But you know that. Only you can't bring yourself to think of anything other than those shitting pigs.

BETT. Dotty –

DOTTY. You don't care a fig about us. Our little lives. That I lost the man I loved. Did you ever read my letters? Did you know we were getting married? Why don't you care? Why don't you ask me how I am? Why don't you ask how Bett's faring? I'm not coming back. You'd have to rip my arm out of its socket before you drag me away.

BETT. Dot –

DOTTY. Who decides if we leave the ATA, Commanding Officer?

C.O. It's your decision. Not mine. Not your father's.

DOTTY. Oh that's good then. Because I say "no". Bett? What do you say? Nothing, probably.

   (**BETT** *is taken aback.*)

BETT. I –

DOTTY. Yes?

BETT. I... Sorry, Dad. I know you need us / but

DOTTY. Well, that's that then. Can I get back to work?

C.O. Of course.

DOTTY. Commander. Thanks for coming to see us, Daddy.

   (**DOTTY** *leaves.*)

BETT. She's broken. I have to stay with her.

   (*Beat.*)

DAD. I wrote a letter. But I didn't post it.

   (**BETT** *looks knowingly.*)

   Look after each other, won't you?

BETT. We will. I will.

   (*She touches his arm as she leaves.*)

DAD. (*Sotto.*) You're doing a grand job.

C.O. I'm sorry, Mr Finlay.

DAD. It's been a long time, Commander. Without my girls. Of course, I know what they're doing here. But if I think about it for more than a moment, I'll...

This is no place for the young. War is a damned thief; stealing our children's youth with no intention of giving it back. I just want them home with me. I want them home.

Scene Four

*(The pub where **JIMMY** works. New Year's Eve, 1944.)*

*(**DOTTY** sings a hit of the time as they all whoop and cheer as **JOY** records it on the wire recorder.*)*

ALL. ENCORE! ANOTHER, ANOTHER!

DOTTY. Sod off! I'm having a drink.

JIMMY. Come on. You've the voice of an angel.

DOTTY. Then you should be paying me for it. I have my rates, you know.

JIMMY. *(As he leaves.)* I'll pay with booze. How's that?

DOTTY. Fine with me. As long as your boss doesn't mind us drinking all the stock?

BETT. Serves them right for leaving Jimmy in charge. Did it work then, Joy?

JOY. *(Checking the recorder.)* I think so. Not sure how you play it without breaking the bloody thing. It's as thin as my Granny's hair.

BETT. I shouldn't muck around with it. I imagine they want it back in one piece.

JOY. Imagine they would if they knew it was gone.

(Beat.)

DOTTY. What?

JOY. What?

---

* A licence to produce *Spitfire Girls* does not include a performance licence for any third-party or copyrighted music. Licensees should create an original composition or use music in the public domain. For further information, please see the Music Use Note on page iii.

BETT. What?

DOTTY. You swiped it?

JOY. Borrowed it.

BETT. From the RAF?!

JOY. I liberated it. My Clive said they wouldn't miss it tonight.

BETT. Your Clive doesn't know his arse from his elbow; they'll be knocking down the door in a minute for stealing government property.

JOY. Give over. It's just a bit of fun and Clive'll take it back next time he comes past this way.

DOTTY. Oh yes, when he pops by on his travels he can just pop it in the back of his bomber before popping back to war, can't he?

JOY. You two. I thought you were more adventurous than this. Stop worrying your little heads. Everything's tickety-boo. Nothing is going to happen.

> *(A loud knock on the door. The three **WOMEN** are startled. Another loud knock. They're motionless. Voices are heard and a door closes loudly. A moment and then **JIMMY** returns.)*

Where the bloody hell did you come from?

JIMMY. Dealing with the riff-raff trying to break in for the hundredth time. Have you not heard the knocking all night?

JOY. Jesus, Mary, Joseph. We thought we were gonners.

JIMMY. Eh?

JOY. Christ alive.

DOTTY. I didn't even notice you'd left.

JIMMY. Charming.

BETT. You'd do well to steer clear of us, Jimmy. We're all likely headed for the slammer.

JIMMY. What are you on about? I've been clearing off punters all night, so we can lock ourselves in.

DOTTY. Well, that's something we'll need to get used to.

(*The three of them laugh.*)

BETT. There's a thief amongst the ranks, Jim.

JOY. And she's taking you all down with her!

JIMMY. Eh? You've all lost your bloody marbles.

DOTTY. Popular game in prison.

(*The three of them laugh again.*)

JIMMY. I'm dimming the lights so we can have this place to ourselves at last.

DOTTY. Oh yes, Jimbo. There's an upside to everything, isn't there? Even a war.

(**JIMMY** *turns some lights off.*)

"Lights – out, inmates!"

(**JOY** *and* **DOTTY** *are beside themselves with laughter.*)

JIMMY. I tell you… It's nice to see that smile of yours, Dotty.

DOTTY. Well, I'm happy, Jimbo… I'm always happy when I'm with my girls. The atta girls. ATA… The Amazing… Three… Aviators. The Abonimable, abonima, abonima, (*Etc.*) abominable… Thieving… Airpersons. The Axtroadinary…oh no, no, no that doesn't work. The Absolutely…

JOY. Trashed Arseholes?

(They laugh.)

DOTTY. Good one, Joy.

JOY. It's better than Always Terrified Airwomen, anyway.

DOTTY. Oh don't get me started.

BETT. She'll get on her soapbox.

JIMMY. I shouldn't take any notice of all that.

DOTTY. We must remember, ladies, we are only temporary articles in this man's world. Aviators Temporarily Available. We must not undermine the military's image of manhood.

BETT. Dot.

DOTTY. No, Betty, I've seen how you've been aping the male pilots, stealing their jobs when clearly "you have not the intelligence to scrub the floor of a hospital properly."

JOY. Oh, that one takes the biscuit.

JIMMY. Who said that?

JOY. Someone wrote a letter to, what? *The Aeroplane* mag?

DOTTY. And the editors felt it was fit to be published.

JOY. Ruddy cheek.

DOTTY. Oh, you wouldn't believe half of them and do you know what makes it worse?

BETT. Can I pilfer a ciggy please, Jim?

DOTTY. Most of the negative / press

JIMMY. Of course / love.

DOTTY. Most of the negative press we've had has come from women. Young women, like us. Jackie had someone accost her in the butchers the other / day

JIMMY. Here you are / Bett.

DOTTY. You won't believe / this.

BETT. Thanks, / love.

DOTTY. And said to her face, to her face, that she was a "bothersome woman who should stick to her cooker and her sewing and leave the men to handle the flying machines". As you can imagine, Jackie told her to stick her cooker where the sun don't shine.

JOY. Pah!

DOTTY. Bett doesn't think we should be quite so outspoken, do you?

BETT. I'm not getting involved.

DOTTY. Do you think I'm outspoken, Joy?

JOY. I think...you...are very pickled.

DOTTY. I am very pickled. But we have to speak our minds. Surely? Otherwise, nothing changes, does it? We keep treading the trodden paths. It's each of us who creates the change. Isn't it? And Jackie did. Last Tuesday. Queuing for tripe.

JIMMY. Beautiful.

DOTTY. We're changing the – the landscape.

JIMMY. Good for her. I mean, for you. For all of you. For all Women. Women everywhere. I love women. All my friends are women. My mum was a woman.

*(They all look at **JIMMY** and snigger.)*

JOY. Sorry, I'm absolutely bursting / here.

DOTTY. Oh for goodness' sake.

JOY. *(Exiting.)* Sorry.

DOTTY. No woman made history by following the rules.

BETT. Don't worry, Dotty. We're breaking them every day up there.

(*They smile and* **DOTTY** *kisses* **BETT**.)

DOTTY. I'll have another, please landlord!

JIMMY. Right you are.

DOTTY. And one for old Joyrider when she comes back.

JIMMY. Comin' up.

DOTTY. He's a good egg.

BETT. It must be nearly midnight, surely?

DOTTY. You got somewhere to be then?

BETT. It's past my bedtime.

DOTTY. Spoilsport.

BETT. We've an early start. It's not like we can just roll into bed, like Jimmy here.

DOTTY. Must be great living and working in the same building.

JIMMY. It'd be alright if it wasn't for you lot coming in every day and smashing up my silence.

DOTTY. We should do it, Bett.

BETT. What?

DOTTY. Run a place like this.

JIMMY. You'd love it, Bett.

DOTTY. When it's all over.

BETT. I don't know.

DOTTY. We could call it "The Queen's Head-ache".

JIMMY. See what you did there.

BETT. Not really that keen on…people.

JIMMY. That's the paradox, love. The solitary landlord with a house full of strangers.

(**JOY** *enters.*)

JOY. What's the time, Mr Wolf?

DOTTY. Time you get this down you.

(She hands her a drink.)

JOY. I think I still have one on the go somewhere.

DOTTY. Then line them up!

JIMMY. *(Looking at his watch.)* Not long ladies. Will you sing us in, Dot?

DOTTY. Oh yes, don't mind if I do, do, do. Once I've nipped to the loo, loo, loo...

(**DOTTY** *exits cracking up at her own joke.*)

JOY. Is she alright?

BETT. I don't know.

JOY. Perhaps you should ask her?

BETT. We don't do that.

JIMMY. Maybe you should?

(Beat.)

All you have to do is ask, Bett.

JOY. Aye, there's no lip to be stiffened between sisters.

BETT. Try saying that quickly.

JOY. *(Fast but perfect.)* There's no lip to be stiffened between sisters.

BETT. Ha! You've not had enough to drink, old chum.

JOY. I'm inclined to agree, old chum.

JIMMY. And it's nearly upon us so let's extract the special reserve from its dark abode.

BETT. Oh no.

JOY. This is where it all goes pear-shaped.

JIMMY. No, no. I think I've nailed it this year. Just you wait.

(**DOTTY** *enters.*)

DOTTY. Did I miss anything?

BETT. No, but you may want to turn back. Jim's just digging out the hard stuff from behind the bar.

DOTTY. This is what I've been waiting for. Chateau Jimmy blanc 1944.

JOY. We can only hope and pray it's better than his '43 reserve.

JIMMY. (*Holding it like a sommelier.*) Here we are, here we are.

BETT. Even the colour of it fills me with dread.

JOY. It does look a wee bit suspect.

DOTTY. Is it meant to be bubbly?

(**JOY** *turns up the radio.*)

JOY. Alright, alright. Stand by chaps. Big Ben's about to ding his dong.

JIMMY. Hang on, shall we set this thing up again?

BETT & DOTTY. Don't touch it!

JIMMY. Stone the crows! Why? Is it rigged?

BETT. Just let Joy deal with it.

DOTTY. Then it's just her fingerprints on the evidence.

JOY. Ta very much chaps.

DOTTY. Here we go!

(**JOY** *records the following. Big Ben chimes.*)

ALL. Ten, nine, eight, seven, six, five, four, three, two, one.

HAPPY NEW YEAR!

DOTTY. *(Sung.)*
SHOULD AULD ACQUAINTANCE BE FORGOT,
AND NEVER BROUGHT TO MIND?
SHOULD AULD ACQUAINTANCE BE FORGOT,
AND DAYS OF AULD LANG SYNE!

FOR AULD LANG SYNE, MY DEAR
FOR AULD LANG SYNE,
WE'LL TAK A CUP O' KINDNESS YET,
FOR AULD LANG SYNE.

> *(During the song. **BETT** takes herself away from the group.)*
>
> *(The others pick up the singing as **DOTTY** takes the bottle of "wine" and joins **BETT** in the quiet.)*

You escaping?

BETT. Only for a moment. You go back.

> *(**DOTTY** plonks herself next to **BETT**.)*

DOTTY. Nope.

BETT. You're sticking with that then?

DOTTY. Can't make me feel any worse.

BETT. "Homemade" makes it sound so cosy.

DOTTY. I know.

BETT. It's lethal. Tastes like something the cat passed.

DOTTY. It's not that bad once you've had a few glasses. You have to commit, keep going until you can no longer taste it. Top up?

BETT. Why not?

DOTTY. Why not indeed. Chin-chin.

BETT. Chin.

> *(They raise their glasses, drink and grimace.)*

DOTTY. Never been one for New Year's, have you?

BETT. Not really.

DOTTY. Why?

BETT. I don't know. It's always made me feel the opposite of how I "should" feel. We're meant to be excited at the prospect of a new year? Fresh beginnings. Togetherness; but it's always made me feel so…

> *(Beat.)*

Perhaps it's just that song.

DOTTY. Yes, I can see that.

BETT. Although you do sing it beautifully.

DOTTY. Why, I thank you.

BETT. Like Mum.

DOTTY. You're not alone, you know. I'll always be here. Whether you like it or not.

BETT. Huh, don't I know. Like a bad smell. A bit like this.

> *(Beat.)*

How about you?

DOTTY. Me?

BETT. Yes.

DOTTY. You know me, I toddle on. Chin up, wings out, fly on.

> *(Beat.)*

DOTTY. I miss him like you wouldn't believe, Bett. But he's gone. Isn't he? We have a job to do. And we don't know how much longer we'll be doing it. So we must make the most of it. I probably shouldn't say this but... I'll miss the war. I will miss it terribly.

I

Have

Loved

Flying.

BETT. Me too, Dot.

DOTTY. The freedom when we step inside an aircraft. Like we can touch the sky with our fingertips. Move the clouds beneath us. Our model train tracks, liquorice roads and toy sheep guiding our way below us. It's a dream, really. Isn't it?

   (**BETT** *smiles.*)

I don't want it to end, Bett. I don't know what I'll do when it's all over.

BETT. Home, I s'pose.

DOTTY. God. "Find a fine young man and settle down my dear".

   (*Beat.*)

BETT. I know, Dot. But you'll be happy again. I promise.

DOTTY. Maybe. Will you?

BETT. Well, that's the age-old question, isn't it? Are we any of us truly happy? How do we know when we are? What if we are but we don't realise it.? What if we find it but smash it to pieces? What if we never find it? What if...?

DOTTY. What?

BETT. What if I've drunk far too much cat piss and I don't know what I'm saying anymore.

(**DOTTY** *laughs.*)

DOTTY. Yes, I'm feeling a bit like that. I'd better head back to my digs.

BETT. Me too. Well, I'll just have one for the road.

(**BETT** *pours another and offers to* **DOTTY**.*)

DOTTY. I'll pass, thanks. Because it may cause me to bring it all up again.

BETT. Get home and get some rest. I'll see you in the morning. Bright and early.

DOTTY. I'll do my best.

BETT. Don't be late tomorrow. The Commander will never let you forget it.

DOTTY. I'll be there. Goodnight, Bett. Happy New Year. Love you.

BETT. Happy New Year, Dotty.

(**DOTTY** *leaves as* **BETT** *joins the other two.*)

Scene Five

*(New Year's Day. 1945. The **COMMANDER**'s office. The **C.O.** is on the phone.)*

C.O. Yes, it's most unlike her. Yup, yup. Well, I'll need to do some re-jigging. We'll make do until she's here.

(A knock at the door.)

Come in!

*(**DOTTY** enters.)*

I must dash. Yup, cheerio.

(She hangs up the phone.)

Still no sign?

DOTTY. It's not like her at all, Commander. I don't know what to say.

C.O. I'm sure the midnight oil was well and truly burnt last night –

DOTTY. Actually, it was not long after midnight I left and she was following on behind me.

C.O. But the rest of you made it on time.

DOTTY. She sometimes takes that shortcut from the pub. What if something…?

C.O. We have a job to do here, Finlay.

DOTTY. It's just so unlike her.

C.O. Dot, I realise you're concerned for Bett but I've an operation to run here and if I don't keep these aircraft moving we will find ourselves, pretty quickly, in the proverbial.

DOTTY. Understood.

C.O. *(Working out the new schedule.)* Now, I had Bett down to pick up a Spit for urgent fittings at Brize Norton so I need to move folk around. Remind me, what's on your chitty this morning?

DOTTY. *(Looking at her Chit.)* A Seafire to Chattis Hill and the Swordfish to Thorney Island.

C.O. *(She takes Dotty's Chit and scribbles on it.)* Right, well someone else can take your Seafire to Chat' Hill when they're back, that's not urgent. You take Bett's Spit this morning, then catch the Anson from Brize Norton. You'll still have plenty of time to get the Swordfish to Thorney Island. Yes. That'll do. *(Handing it back to* **DOTTY**.*)* This is a Mark II Spit, Finlay so open up the throttle gently else the yaw will bite you, so be / ready for the swing.

DOTTY. / ready for the swing. Noted. Thank you, Commander.

C.O. It won't go unnoticed.

DOTTY. Thank you, Commander. You'll keep an eye out for Bett?

C.O. I will.

DOTTY. I'm sorry, Commander.

C.O. Not your fault, Finlay, but if you see her before I do...

DOTTY. Yes, Commander.

C.O. Blue Skies.

DOTTY. Blue Skies.

*(***DOTTY** *leaves.)*

Scene Six

(Bett's pub. The early hours of New Year's Day, 1960. It's still raining. **BETT** *sits in the dark smoking and drinking. She has a bottle of "wine" next to her. There is a knock at the door.)*

BETT. We're closed!

(Another knock. **BETT** *looks at her watch and goes to the door, unlocks it;* **FRANK**'s *there.)*

Blimey. What is it, Frank?

FRANK. I forgot them shoes.

BETT. You forgot the shoes. I knew you'd forget the shoes.

FRANK. Forget my head, wouldn't I, love.

BETT. You could've come in the morning though, Frank. Not trudged back here in the pelting rain. Do you realise what time it is?

FRANK. Yup. Ah. Well. I'm here now.

BETT. There they are.

FRANK. Ta, love. You're very kind.

BETT. I'm not, Frank. I just don't like seeing little kids in worn-out shoes.

FRANK. Right-o, love.

BETT. Make sure these ones find their way to his feet, eh?

FRANK. They will.

BETT. And they don't go walkies like the last pair.

FRANK. They won't, they won't.

BETT. They'd better not. Or I'll stop serving you, Frank.

FRANK. Alright, Bett no need for the drastic action. Speaking of which, any chance of a snifter?

(Beat.)

BETT. You're lucky to have him, you know.

FRANK. I know, love.

BETT. I'm not sure you do, Frank. Else you wouldn't have him sit out there in broken shoes whilst you drink his childhood away in here. He's a lovely little boy and I don't want to see him sitting on this stool in twenty years. Go on, get off. You've not been home five minutes before leaving the poor kid on his own again.

FRANK. He's alright.

BETT. Is he?

FRANK. Yes, yes. Barb's back now.

BETT. Good. Go on then, Frank. Go home.

FRANK. Right-o, love.

*(He turns to go. He looks back at **BETT** who is sitting and smoking. Long pause.)*

She gone now, has she?

BETT. Eh?

FRANK. She let you be?

BETT. What?

(Beat.)

FRANK. I see you. I know you think I'm a drunk and no good to nobody.

BETT. I –

FRANK. No, no, no. You've just said as much. But I see things. I see your sadness.

FRANK. And every New Year's Eve a strange little veil falls over you. Others don't see it. But I do. And I see you talking. She gone now?

> (**BETT** *looks.*)

BETT. How do you…?

> (*Pause.* **FRANK** *smiles.*)

I s'pose

I should've gotten over it by now

Pulled myself together

But I can't seem to

I can't stop

> (*Beat.*)

Ah well.

"Chin up, wings out, fly on"…

FRANK. I know, love. It's bloody hard. I know.

BETT. What the hell do you know? You weren't there. I wasn't there. I wasn't there. I wasn't bloody there –

> (*Silence as* **FRANK** *looks at her and then kindly touches her hand.*)

Don't sell those shoes, Frank. Promise me you won't sell those shoes.

FRANK. I won't –

BETT. If I see your little boy –

FRANK. I won't.

> (**BETT** *and* **FRANK** *look at each other.*)

Tell her. Next time. Tell her.

(**BETT** *looks.*)

Right-o then, love. I best get back and get some shut-eye before Jack wakes me up with the early morning death stare. Night, love.

(He goes to leave.)

BETT. Shoes!

FRANK. Oh, bloody hell.

(He turns back and picks them up.)

Cheero.

*(**FRANK** leaves. Silence except for the rain easing.)*

BETT. Why did you have to take it? Why? Why?

(Beat.)

It was my fault –

*(**DOTTY** appears in the shadows behind **BETT**. **BETT** does not look at her.)*

DOTTY. No Bett –

BETT. It was my fault –

DOTTY. It was an accident –

BETT. I was late –

DOTTY. No. It could've happened to any of us. The weather was fine when I left. I set off at zero nine hundred hours. On the dot. But it changed pretty quickly as I made my way north. I didn't make it to Brize Norton. Lost sight somewhere over the Downs. Just couldn't find a gap in the clouds. The Spitfire was my most wonderful companion up until that day. I crash-landed in a farmer's field just west of Newbury and the Spit burst into flames. Our blue skies coated in black smoke.

BETT. I'm so sorry, Dotty. It should've been –

DOTTY. No.

> *(Beat.)*

BETT. You're more alive than I am. I'm the solitary landlady with a house full of ghosts.

> *(Beat.)*

I can't keep answering the door to you.

DOTTY. Then don't, Betty.

> *(Pause.)*

BETT. I hate you. I bloody hate you. I hate you for not landing that Spitfire. You'd done it a thousand times and you were a far better pilot than I ever was so why couldn't you land the damned thing? But then. You always were bloody selfish; thinking that your decisions had no consequences. But here I am. Stuck here. Still waiting for you to knock on the soddin' door. I hate you. For saying that you'll always be next to me because you're not. Are you?

DOTTY. I'm so sorry.

BETT. Are you? Or is that me?

> *(Beat.)*

I think you'd better go.

> *(**DOTTY** starts to move away.)*

Tom… I think I –

> *(Beat.)*

But I loved you more.

*(**DOTTY** disappears. It's stopped raining. The birds are murmuring and perhaps we see a chink of light coming through.)*

Dot?

Dotty?

*(**BETT** sees she is alone.)*

Happy New Year, Dotty. Blue skies.

*(**BETT** raises her glass and drinks. She grimaces.)*

Good God. Still tastes like cat piss.

(She sits back as it gets brighter and the morning chorus swells.)

(Blackout.)